Letters to Gulab

Letters to Gulab is more than a collection of poems; it's a quiet place to rest, to feel, and to heal. These pages carry the author's softness, rage, grief, and growth. You will find pieces of love, loss, longing, and resilience gently woven into every line. This book is a reflection of everything Manvi Bhandari has been and everything she is still becoming. But more than anything, it's an offering for the days your own heart feels too tired, too full, or too quiet. If you find a part of yourself in these words, hold it close. It was always meant to find you.

Letters to Gulab

Manvi Bhandari

AMARYLLIS

AMARYLLIS
An imprint of Manjul Publishing House Pvt. Ltd.
• C-16, Sector 3, Noida, Uttar Pradesh 201 301, India
Website: www.manjulindia.com
Registered Office:
• 2nd Floor, Usha Preet Complex, 42 Malviya Nagar,
Bhopal 462 003 – India
Distribution Centres
Ahmedabad, Bengaluru, Chennai, Hyderabad,
Kochi, Kolkata, Mumbai, Noida, Pune

Letters to Gulab by Manvi Bhandari

This hardback edition first published in India in 2026

ISBN 978-93-7317-234-7

Printed and bound in India by Thomson Press (India) Ltd.

Contents

*The book contains discussions about mental health, suicide, death, and other such sensitive topics, which some readers may find difficult to read.

To Saanvi and Shailja, thank you for being my favorite poems.

Letter to You

dear reader,

if you managed to pick this book up, i want you to know that what you hold in the hollow of your palms is far more than paper and ink. you are now holding my heart in your palms. with each word, my heart beats and speaks of anger, love, infinitude, confusion, and all the feelings i've found too hard to carry over the years.
i hope that with each word you read, with each syllable that installs itself between the space in your ribs, with each rhyme that swivels inside you for days to come, you think of me. the weight of knowing i bestow upon you; the living, breathing testimony to my existence and my art.

i hope you fall in love with these words the way i did. i hope you find tender comfort between these lines like i did. but most of all, i hope you find in me, a friend.
the human heart is fragile, bruised, but an artwork of a life that has been lived. i hope you learn to love it.

Acknowledgements

to my forever favorite human, my hero, my very best friend and my great-grandmother, Usha Bhandari.

some people teach through words, but you taught through the way you lived. with kindness, patience, and an unshakable strength, you showed me that the greatest lesson isn't found in books but in the way we carry ourselves. of all the things you taught me, the most precious was how to be myself. in a world that constantly asks us to change, you made sure i knew the power of staying true.

more than a teacher, you were my childhood. you were the warmth in my earliest memories, the gentle voice that made everything feel safe. you were home before i even knew what that word meant. and though time moves forward and life carries me to new places, i will always carry a piece of you with me woven into the way i speak, the way i love, the way i stand tall even when the world feels heavy.

if somehow you see me from up there, i hope you can smile. i hope you know that every word i write and every dream i chase, is because of you. you may not be here to turn the pages with me, but this book, this piece of my heart will always belong to you.

with all my love and gratitude,
your manu

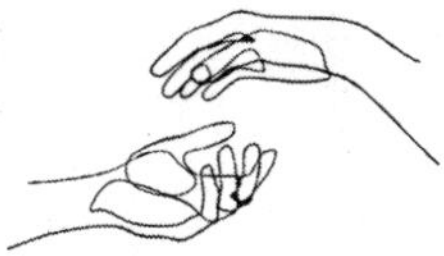

Fixer

i'm not sure how to fix the world's problems,
but somehow, i'm certain i'm supposed to try.
when i was young, i learned that my own wounds
always came second to the feet
that needed a rug to walk upon.
when you grow up a fixer,
you forget how to be anything else.
you start to believe the sky exists
only so you can hold it up.
but as you get older,
the sky stretches wider,
heavier than the strength
you were ever meant to carry alone.

Mirror

oh dear mirror,
when did you become such an enemy?
when did looking at you become so draining?
when did you start to show the worst of me?
oh dear mirror,
when did the tiny shard of your pointed glass
puncture my skin,
not deep enough to bleed,
but just enough to remind me i am breakable?
when did your reflection start whispering lies,
or worse
start telling the truth i cannot bear to hear?
oh dear mirror,
were you always this cruel,
or did i simply learn to see myself through your eyes

Wedding Dress

i'm terrified i'll still miss you
in my wedding dress,
i'm terrified of hearing
the echoes of our laughs
from all the years that took you from me
i'm terrified because as i'll walk down the aisle
my wrist will feel bare
and sting of your absence holding me back
i'm so terrified i'll look around the room
search for the only eyes i could ever love,
i'm terrified i'll look for you
in every crowd, every hall
every stranger, every noise
i'm terrified that i'll still miss you
i'll still hold onto you
i'll still look for you
even when i shouldn't
i'm terrified i will forever feel incomplete
i am so terrified
because what's more terrifying
than loving someone you don't have?

Wilted Flowers

do you remember our conversation about wilted flowers,
how we traced the veins of dying petals,
calling them maps of where love had been?
you said decay was just another kind of poetry,
that even in falling apart, things still whisper their past
the way old books smell of dust and memory,
the way autumn trees burn gold before they bare their bones.
i watched a rose collapse in slow surrender,
its blush fading like a lover's last word,
but wasn't there something gentle in its unraveling?
something soft in the way it let go? we are all wilting, aren't we?
a little more with each passing sun,
but maybe that is where beauty lingers
not in holding on, but in knowing when to bloom,
when to fade, when to finally rest.
so when the flowers in your hands begin to droop,
don't mourn them
press them between pages, let them live in poetry,
let them teach you that even in decay,
there is grace.

Lessons to Learn

you were my person,
my home, my rest.
and now, you're my favorite lesson
the kind that carves itself into my bones,
that lingers long after the page has turned.
you were a hard lesson,
the kind that breaks me just to teach me,
the kind i wish i never had to learn,
and yet, with every breath i take,
i still love you like i haven't.

Someday

someday, we will go back to being just strangers
someday, the spark in your eyes
when you talk about my smile
will die
fade into a loose shrug
someday, when this woven shadow
falls behind,
someday when talking about me doesn't seem too tough,
someday when we will just be two broken halves of a future we could never hold,
you will probably forget me
my touch on your warm skin
will fall cold
and all that'll remain
of a love, far too young
is a void we can't feel
and you won't think of me
not until one day
when the sun burns your skin
the wind erodes the broken pieces
and you see

what all we could be
carved on bones and under skins
a few promises, untouched by time
and a story too cruel to call mine
i like to believe, i'll come back to your mind
stand beside you for that while
and maybe, you'll think,
you never really forgot me
the touch on your skin,
covered by foreign hands,
my voice drowned by others
and the laugh, a faint echo you could only hear
if you stayed quite too long.
the shadow, never really left
and under all those years and lies
i'm still in the backseat of your mind

Scars

it's called healing,
but healing that leaves scars
because when the body bleeds,
the mind doesn't.
when my veins scream,
my thoughts whisper,
and for a moment,
the war inside me falls silent.
i have never felt more alive
than in the moments
i feel myself slipping away,
as if the closer i come to the edge,
the lighter the weight on my chest becomes.
but tell me,
what kind of healing
feels like dying?

I Deserved a Goodbye

i'm not upset that you left.
i'm upset that you never said goodbye,
never gave me a warning,
never let me know it was the last time.
i was counting on you,
believing you'd show,
holding space for you like a fool
but you turned me into a punchline
without delivering the joke.
i'm not upset that you left,
but damn,
i'm furious you left me waiting.

Love of Knives

your abuse feels like love
because you convinced me it was.
and starving people eat anything,
even poison wrapped in pretty words,
even knives disguised as an embrace.
i swallowed every apology like it could fill me,
held onto every "i love you" like it was nourishment,
but love is not supposed to leave you hollow,
not supposed to taste like blood.
i was starving
so i ate what you gave me.
but i am hungry no more.

Heartbreak Doesn't Write Poetry

they say heartbreak writes better than the poet,
that it grips the pen tighter,
bleeds sharper,
fills the pages with more ruin than the poet ever could.
but they are wrong.
heartbreak does not write the poet,
the poet writes heartbreak.
it does not hold the pen
the poet does, steady and unshaken.
heartbreak does not shape the poet.
it is the poet who takes heartbreak,
crushes it between his palms,
and turns it into something worth reading.

Absence

i hope my absence gives you the peace my love couldn't.
but i also hope it haunts you,
carves into you the way your love carved into me.
i hope it lingers like an ache in your chest,
a phantom pain you can't reach.
i hope it twists the knife,
rips through you the way your words once did,
leaves you gasping in the silence
where my voice used to be.
i hope my absence gives you peace
but not before it destroys you first.

All My Ghosts

all my ghosts
chase you,
because you hold the pieces of me
they could never keep.
you wear my laughter like it belongs to you,
carry my softness in the palms of your hands,
speak my name like it never tasted like sorrow.
they follow you,
hungry, restless
because you have the love
they spent years trying to take.

To the Little Girl in Me

to the little girl in me,
i know you're still there.
i feel you in the way my smile lingers,
hear you in the way my laughter escapes,
light and unguarded.
little girl,
don't be scared.
i know you tremble when people leave,
flinch at the sound of footsteps fading,
but you are not lost.
you are still here,
woven into every soft moment,
every quiet joy,
every time someone chooses to stay.

My Mother Once Told Me

my mother once told me
she wanted me to be like the sun.
i asked her why.
did she want me to shine bright,
to rise high,
to be something the whole world looked up to?
she smiled, shook her head.
"no," she said.
"i want you to be like the sun because no matter who turns away,
no matter who closes their blinds,
no matter who refuses to see you,
you will keep burning.
you will keep rising.
you will keep going."

Feminine?

a year earlier
i found it rather an insult to be feminine
to be feminine, i thought, was to be weak
to be feminine, i thought, was to not be able to speak
to be feminine, i thought, was to always bend, never grow.
i didn't understand the meaning of feminine
to be feminine was not to have pretty as an afterthought,
not to shrink myself into something delicate,
not to soften my voice to make space for another's.
a year ago, i mistook femininity for fragility,
thought strength had to be loud,
thought power had to be sharp,
thought softness meant surrender.
but now, i see it in the way a mother carries the weight of the world
with hands that still know how to be gentle,
in the way a woman stands tall
even when the world tries to fold her in half.
to be feminine is to be fire and water,
to be tender without breaking,
to hold grace in one hand and defiance in the other.

it is not weakness.
it is not silence.
it is not bending without growing.
to be feminine is to be whole
a force, a presence, a power all its own

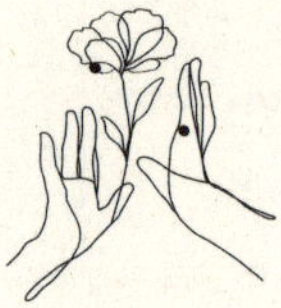

Stay

you don't want to live, you said,
but do you really want to go today?
and if you do, i'll hold you,
i'll say goodbye
but you've always loved the rain.
so why not stay a little longer?
it's already cloudy.
we could sit outside,
let the water soak through our skin.
and when it stops,
if you still want to go,
i'll find the other five men
while you take your pill.
but if you get too cold,
come inside, dry off,
watch a show you've never seen.
if, by the third episode,
you still want to leave,
take a knife and go with a smile.
but if the cliffhanger is too much,
watch another season, maybe two.

and why leave on an empty stomach?
we could get pizza,
you could talk,
we could waste time.
i won't ask you to stay forever,
just for the night.
and maybe in the morning,
you could slip away with the sunlight.
but a morning death is too cliché,
isn't it?
so wait for noon.
we'll have ice cream,
talk a little more.
and if you still want to go,
i'll pick the perfect casket
and flowers you won't even care for.
but guess what?
it's a full moon tonight.
you love those.
call your mom, your dad, your brother.
if they don't listen,
then sure,
die beneath the moonlight
or maybe stay.
because your lungs still have air.
your heart still beats.
and if living feels too much,
just breathe.
just exist.
just stay.

one more day.
because if you really want to go,
you will, i promise.
but does it have to be today?
suicide has always felt so cliché.
so stay.
find a good book,
i'll make the coffee.
stay this one life,
stay with me.
because i can't find the five men,
and you don't even like flowers.
so what's the point of a casket
when there are still a few reasons to stay?

Right Where You Left Me

(Manvi's Version)

hair turn grey
and the wine grows finer
dust on my feet,
holding me to my seat
i fill my throat with aged wine
so it doesn't get to speak truths
break perfect delusions of you
my throat filled with wine
so i don't hear you're out
with a wife and your child
my hands with dust
into my lungs
i take fewer breaths
as i become faint in your memory
and take another sip of my wine
right where you left me.

It's Time to Go

(Manvi's Version)

clock ticks
that hollow feeling
eating at your chest
you try to hear our laughs
the same we shared
every night
but they grow fainter
and you search for the last bit
of home in me
that you seemed to know so very well
but when the clock strikes midnight
you can feel your bones grow tight
and you know
in your soul
it's time to go.

Tolerate It

(Manvi's Version)

a poet's love
is celebrated
but in all my pages
i hate to freely admit it
my muse doesn't celebrate
my quotes
about his eyes
his smile
his breath
a poet's love is celebrated
and then somehow
my muse seems to simply
tolerate it.

Champagne Problems

(Manvi's Version)

i don't hold hands anymore
you wouldn't understand why
and i pray as i hope
i can't remember all my
champagne problems
but every ball dance
when you reach for my palm
i take it away
like it were cursed
you come close and whisper
i shut my ears
you won't understand
my champagne problems.

Lipstick and Heels

when i was five, my mother gave me her perfume
to play dress-up.
it was almost empty anyway.
i would spritz it on, tilt my chin up,
pretend to be her
the way her scent lingered long after she left a room,
as if she carried warmth in the air itself.
when i was ten, she handed me her red lipstick
to wear to an event.
it was nearly finished anyway.
i pressed it onto my lips,
practiced a smile in the mirror,
pretended to be her
the way she spoke with such certainty,
as if the world made space for her words.
when i turned twelve,
she gave me her heels, her dresses, her jewelry.
i put them on,
desperate to step into the shape of her,
to be something close,
something resembling.

but at thirteen, when she gave me her perfume,
her lipstick, her heels
this time for my own birthday,
i stood in front of the mirror
and didn't even try to be like her.
because i know now
it isn't the perfume that makes my mother unforgettable,
it's not the lipstick that gives her power,
not the heels that make her stand tall.
i can wear her perfume,
leave traces of my scent in every room,
but it isn't her scent that lingers
it's her essence.
i can paint my lips red,
but it isn't the color that commands attention
it's her words.
now, as fourteen approaches,
my inner child still wears her perfume
not to become her,
but to feel her near,
to learn from her.
because i know i will never be her.
but if i can be even a little close,
that feels enough for now.

When I Was

when i was 3,
i didn't think about turning 5.
but i thought it would be cool
i could raise five fingers,
and that would be my age.
there was something simple about it,
something easy.
at 5, the world seemed bigger,
the rules a little looser,
the fun a little louder.
when i was 5,
i didn't think about turning 7.
but i thought it would be cool
i could raise five fingers and two more,
and that would be my age.
seven felt important,
like a step toward something greater.
there was so much more you could do at 7.
when i was 7,
i didn't think about turning 9.
but i thought it would be cool

five fingers on one hand, four on the other.
a little closer to something new,
something older,
something just out of reach.
when i was 9,
i didn't think about turning 11.
but i thought it would be cool
i wouldn't need my fingers anymore.
instead of showing my age,
i could say it,
let the number roll off my tongue
like a quiet kind of pride.
11 meant something.
there was so much more you could do at 11.
when i was 11,
i didn't think about turning 13.
but i thought it would be cool
to finally be a teenager,
to wear the title like a badge,
to step into something bigger than childhood.
13 meant freedom,
meant growth,
meant more.
but now, at 13,
i don't think about turning 15.
i don't think it will be cool.
i will say my age,
and people will expect more.
more responsibility,
more understanding,

more than i might be ready to give.
and somewhere along the way,
i have realized
staying 3, wanting nothing more,
was having the most of all.

28th June 2010

June 28, 2010
the day i was born.
somewhere, a tree began growing with me.
she will turn 14 soon.
i wonder if she knows
i have been growing beside her all this time.
do her branches bend the way my limbs do?
does she stretch toward the sky like the dreams i hold inside me?
is she small like my body,
or does she tower like the thoughts i can't contain?
when autumn comes,
does she fight to keep her leaves,
afraid of being bare,
afraid of losing the ones who once clung to her,
who made her feel whole?
does winter make her shiver?
or does she stand strong,
rooted in the quiet ache of waiting for spring?
when birds come for her sap,
do they drink her dry,
or do they get caught in the weight of what she holds?

does she grow a new ring for every year i survive?
does she wear her scars the way i wear mine?
does she peel her bark,
trying to shed the parts of herself she doesn't want,
the way i pick at my skin in the mirror?
when it rains,
does she let it wash over her,
or does she drown beneath the weight of it?
June 28, 2024
she will be 14.
i will be 14.
i wonder if she feels it too.

Soundtrack of Your Backseat

April 2024, i'm getting ready to go out with my friends.
"will you be home for dinner?" mum asks.
"yeah, no i'll be back by 7."
and as i sit in my car, it starts raining.
the kind of rain that blurs the windshield,
the kind that makes you pause for just a second.
i turn on the radio, flipping through static,
and then i hear it,
my favorite song from 2015.
the one that played in the backseat of my mother's car,
the one she sang along to while i watched the raindrops race down the glass.
i don't know the last time we drove to the store together.
i don't know the last time i let her pick the music,
the last time i sang with her.
i don't know when i got too old
to sit in the passenger seat and talk about my week.
but i do know this,
she was right.
someday came quietly,
and i got older,

and somewhere along the way,
the backseat became empty.
i check the time.
6:32 p.m.
dinner will be ready soon.
i cancel the plans,
turn the car around,
and drive home.

Pretty Boy

i never thought love had a voice
until i heard his laugh
light, unshaken, the kind that stays with you.
his eyes held me
like my mother's embrace,
gentle, knowing, safe.
his warmth ran through me
like the words i've underlined a hundred times,
the ones that feel like home.
"pretty boy,"
my mother calls him,
and pretty he is
like the poems i never finished,
the moon i never quite captured,
the fleeting kind of beauty
that lingers long after it's gone.
"he is a pretty boy,"
i tell her one evening,
and i smile, because i know.
she smiles back,
because she knows too.

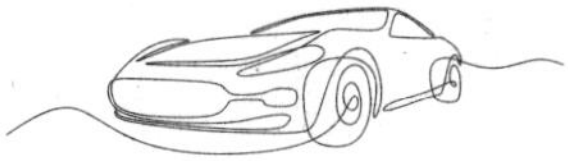

Backseat of Your Car

i was seven and in the backseat of my mum's car when my favorite song played on the radio. as the lyrics i loved so dearly stumbled into my ears, panic settled deep in my chest, the kind of panic that comes from knowing something beautiful is about to end. what if the song stopped before i could hear it all the way through? what if our stop came too soon, cutting off the melody before it reached the part i loved most? i held my breath, as if time might stretch itself just for me, just this once. staring out the window, i watched the world blur by, wondering how something so perfect, so fleeting could slip away without anyone else noticing. the chorus played, my heart raced, and i whispered the words like a prayer, as if singing them softly enough could make them last forever. but then, the music faded, the car slowed, and silence settled in. i was seven, and for the first time, i understood that even the things we love the most will leave before we're ready.

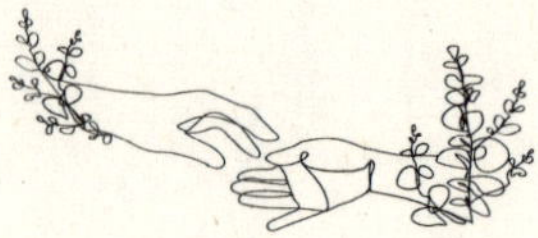

Maybe a Bad Person

maybe a bad person
or maybe just 15
because no,
i promise
the world doesn't end with your mistakes
and the world doesn't burn for your sins
a flower blooms and i think you miss
the beauty of growth
maybe a bad person,
or maybe just 15
because regret feels heavier
when you're still learning
how to carry yourself.
no,
i promise,
the world doesn't end
with your mistakes,
the sky doesn't fall
just because your hands
shook when you held it.
the world doesn't burn

for your sins,
only for the ones
who never tried to change.
a flower blooms,
soft, steady,
reaching toward the light,
and i think you miss
the beauty of growth,
how even the broken things
still find a way
to rise.

Twenty-Four Hours

so when we talk about hours,
you say
you spent six asleep,
woke up,
cried because of your dream,
heard me somewhere
between the echoes and the quiet,
then spent two in the shower,
trying to wash off a feeling
that never quite leaves.
you spent four staring at the ceiling,
blinking at the weight of existence,
two more convincing yourself
to get out of bed,
and three scrolling through a world
that never stops moving,
even when you do.
you spent one trying to eat,
but the food tasted like nothing,
and another pacing the room,
searching for something

you were never sure existed.
then there were the hours
you won't count,
the ones spent drowning in a silence
so loud it swallowed you whole.
and when I ask about your day,
you just say,
"nothing much."

Scarlet Letters

scarlet letters
unfinished novels
and i promise you
the poetry was better
than the scandal.
whispers in ink,
secrets pressed between pages,
a love story abandoned
mid-sentence
and i promise you,
the poetry was softer
than the silence that followed,
gentler than the hands
that tore us apart.
scarlet letters fade,
unfinished novels gather dust,
but the words,
the words still burn.

The Funny Thing is

i'm still waiting for the punchline.
for someone to step in, to say, just kidding,
to shake me awake from this cruel trick.
please, take all my hope,
grind it down to dust,
scatter it where even the wind won't find it.
because if you don't,
i'll keep waiting
and waiting
for the joke to land,
for the laughter to start,
for the ache in my chest to mean something
other than emptiness.
and the funny thing is
when it finally hits,
when the silence stretches too long,
when the echoes of a joke never told
ring louder than the truth
i'll laugh so hard
i'll shatter,
i'll break open at the seams,

and maybe then you'll tell me
it was all just a joke, right?
funny thing is
even if this was never real,
even if this was all just smoke and mirrors,
i have never felt more hollow.
and maybe one day,
i'll learn to laugh about it.
maybe the punchline will go:
"and the funny thing is
she was the only one who didn't get the joke."

We Will Meet Again

we will meet again someday
but i won't be fourteen anymore
with a heart that only yearns for you
we will meet again someday
but this time
my lungs won't ache
for every breath you are not near
my heart won't break for every fate
that binds us here
we will meet again someday
but this time
my hands won't tremble
at the thought of letting go
my dreams won't shatter
under the weight of what we could have been
we will meet again someday
but i will not be the same
no longer waiting, no longer longing
just a quiet smile, a nod in passing
two souls who once burned,
now only embers in the wind

Happy Birthday

when i send you a
"happy birthday" text,
will your heart skip a beat, will your lips curl into a smile, will you
shake it off, put your phone away,
and smile at the friend next to you?
will you think about how i remembered,
how i will always remember, how that date stays etched in my mind,
like the most beautiful set of numbers
perfectly aligned.
will you think of leaving a piece of cake for me,
knowing i'll never be there to eat it, but still keeping it aside, because
you know if we were still us, i'd get the first bite.
and then, will you decide, to text me back just a "thank you," devoid
of any emoticon, stripped of exclamation marks, full stops, commas,
because even punctuations didn't have it in them to hold us together.
and you'll hope i never reply,
and i won't.
and we'll wait,
for seven months to pass, for my birthday to arrive, and i'll stare at
my phone, holding my breath,
"happy birthday."

and just like that, birthdays will become our thing
a reminder.
a quiet ritual
a silent ritual
we won't call,
we won't ask how the other has been,
but somewhere, in the spaces between those words, between "happy" and "birthday," between sending and receiving, we'll know we were here, once.

The Boys Will Make You Cry

the boys will make you cry
some with words they never meant,
some with hands too quick to leave,
some with love that burns too fast
and leaves you standing in the ash.
some will teach you how to wait,
how to twist yourself in knots,
how to give and bend and break
for someone who won't meet you there.
some will love you like a fleeting song,
sweet but gone before the end,
some will never love at all,
only the way you make them feel.
but one day, a man will come
who holds your heart like something rare,
who does not leave you guessing, waiting,
who loves you steady, loves you there.
yes, the boys will make you cry
but so will love that's true,
because hearts that never ache or break
are hearts that never beat for two.

I Lost a Brother Today

i lost a brother today
not to earth, nor fire, nor fate,
but to the slow decay of knowing
someone who no longer knows you.
i lost a brother today
once, we spoke in sleepless laughter,
in echoes that filled the space between stars,
in promises too young to break
but even the sky is not forever.
i lost a brother today
not in one sharp, shattering moment,
but in the quiet erosion of meaning,
in the space between words unspoken,
in the way his name feels different in my mouth.
i lost a brother today
watched him slip into a world
where i no longer belong,
where the air is thin with expectation,
where the weight of becoming
is heavier than the weight of remembering.
i lost a brother today

and maybe he lost me too,
but neither of us will say it,
so instead, we pretend,
call it life, call it growing,
call it anything but grief.

No One Makes My Mom Laugh as Much as My Dad

when she was three, she watched her mom
fold laundry in the kitchen, her fingers slow,
picking up socks, matching them like puzzle pieces,
while her dad hummed in the hallway below.
he'd always hum when he thought she wasn't listening
not the song, just a tune, like he was too happy
to keep it inside.
and then, her mom's laugh,
like a soft wind through the old oak tree,
spilled into the room, warm and sure,
when her dad cracked his favorite joke
again, the one about the shoes.
she heard it every day,
but it never got old, not to her mom.
"no one makes my mom laugh as much as my dad,"
she whispered to her dolly,
watching them from the corner of the kitchen door,
as they danced, carefully,
like the floor beneath them
might remember the years they'd spent together.
her dad's hands on her mom's waist,

so gentle, as if time had made them
fragile, but still strong.
when she was seven,
she watched them sit on the porch at night,
each with a cup of tea, no sugar,
the steam swirling in the air like a secret.
they didn't need to speak;
their silence was something to hold,
like a soft blanket shared between two hearts.
she'd curl her fingers around the railing,
imagining she was holding onto them,
into the quiet forever.
at ten, she watched them paint the fence
together in the backyard,
her mom smudging white paint
on the end of her nose,
and her dad laughing again,
the same laugh that had filled their house
since before she was born,
before the old couch had worn down its fabric
and the lamp had flickered for the hundredth time.
and at fifteen,
when her world felt bigger and louder,

she saw them again,
mom and dad, sitting side by side,
holding hands on the couch,
like no one could touch them,
like no one had ever touched them.
their fingers intertwined like the roots of a tree
that had grown, unbroken, through storms and seasons.
she wasn't sure what love was,
not in the way they could understand,
but when she looked at them
her mom, soft-eyed and full of warmth,
and her dad, a quiet strength beside her,
she knew that some things,
the things that mattered most,
never needed words to say them.
it was in the way they didn't hurry anymore,
the way they knew the small things held the world:
her mom's smile as she folded his shirts,
the way her dad's laugh filled every space
he touched,
and the way her parents grew older together,
hand in hand,
as if there was nowhere else
they would ever need to be.

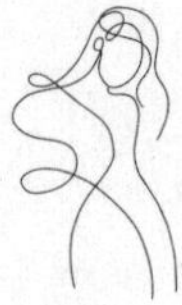

Flesh and Phantom

i wear the weight of you
in the curve of my spine,
in the spaces between my ribs
you're here,
but not here.
flesh and phantom,
woven together
in a fabric of what-ifs
and old prayers never answered.
the night you left,
you didn't say goodbye.
you folded into my shadow,
a secret stitched into my skin.
i search for you in the reflection
of city streets and rising mist
but you're always out of reach,
a name lost to wind,
an imprint in dust.
your touch still lingers
the way it felt when your fingers traced
the map of my scars,

the pressure of your absence
pushing against my chest.
flesh and phantom
two halves of the same myth.
i carry you in forgotten songs
we used to sing in the dark,
each note a ghost
that clings to my throat
whenever i try to speak your name.
and so i walk with you,
each footstep a negotiation
between who i've become
and the phantom of who i used to be.
i'm not sure which one is real,
but i know i'm bound to both,
like a prayer bound to its god,
like the sea is bound to the shore
even as it erodes it.

Meri Gulab

the rose has lost its bloom,
you've settled gently into earth's embrace,
the petals fall, no longer bright, no room,
for vibrant life, now wrapped in quiet grace,
the slumber calls, and you have found your place.
meri gulab,
your fragrance fills the air,
but no more laughter, no more tender sound.
the rose is still, as though it's always there,
but underneath, the silence wraps around,
and in the stillness, love can still be found.
meri gulab,
you've gone where roses go,
where thorns don't hurt, and time has lost its fight.
your spirit rests where only softness flows,
the garden quiet, beneath the moon's pale light,
a peace that comes, without a tear in sight.

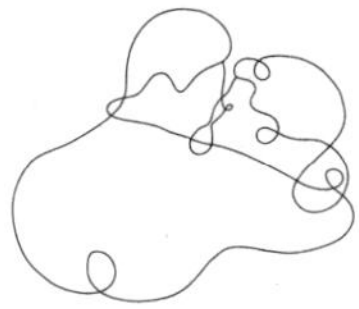

Were You Talking to Me?

"were you talking to me?"
i said, you sounded so strange
"look over me from the afterlife"
my voice cracked and you barely smiled
but you held my finger
like i held yours on my first night
and you brushed my hair
like i brushed yours when you died
and i lay in your lap
before you lay down to sleep
and i told you i'll miss you
you're what i wish i could keep
but you tell me death is a gift
and life is a lesson
a picture album, a watch and an old ring
all to my name
all lessons i'll carry to my own grave
and when the sun shines too bright
or when the rain isn't too cold
or when the wind doesn't mess my hair
i'll look at you and say hello

and when the tears dry
the house goes empty
i'll lay in your bed, maybe twice a week
something for old times sake
and i'll tell you my mistakes
maybe this time it won't seem so unfair
but death is a gift and life is a lesson,
that's what you said
so when your heart goes silent
mine will beat for you
make the most of this lesson
when i'll see you again,
i'll give you a story to tell

No Revenge

no revenge
because someday the smoke from your cigar
will settle and
i'll not be across the fog
someday when the dusty air
you inhale fills your bare lungs
you'll taste, on your tongue
the guilt of us
and your lungs feel empty
the absence of me
someday when the warmth from the burning cigarette
falls cold
you'll realize how terribly alone
you stand somewhere far
far from me, far from home
no revenge because as you purchase another box of cigarettes
you will look around you
so desperately to see me
in empty eyes of strangers
and i won't be there
someday when your last cigarette

finishes,
my voice will echo
linger in your ears
like the smoke
lingers at your breath
all your worst fears
settle on the ground
next to your smoke
is this what you are?
all alone?
a demon of confinement
all your bones
all words you've said
engraved like a curse
a sour, bitter taste
not from your smoke
from a guilt you can't suppress
no revenge
because someday
this is who you will be
this is you,
and you are everything you never wanted to see.

Dear Dove

dear dove,
come and sit
come and bleed
let me admire your hair
admire the way you breathe
five more minutes,
five only, please
dear dove,
too much, i won't ask
a few questions
ones i don't think you'll have the answers to
dear dove,
sit with me while we still have the sun
"too much to learn from"
you'd say,
fifteen and too much to live for
dear dove, won't you save me
look at me
stay with me, bleed with me
dear dove, five more minutes
five only, please.

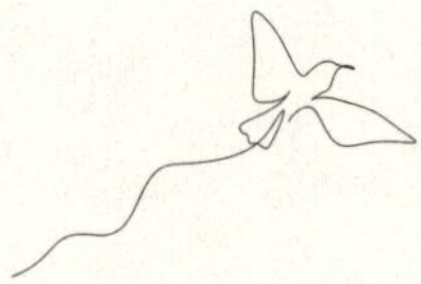

Dear Dove (Part 2)

dearest dove,
a year i see before me
a year we've not stained
of sins we're too young to claim
dear dove,
before the moment's gone
sit. stay. is all i'll ask
dove, won't you lay?
in my lap where the warmth of my embrace
meets yours
dove, won't you stay?
caress my palm
trace the lines of our fate
and then with the same eyes
you'd have to tell me you can't stay
oh, dearest dove,
how i wish i could tie these broken bones
to yours, tie your soul to mine
dearest dove, i wish you could stay the night
but i can't hold these feathers
these feathers of flight,

so, my dove,
go and soar
for i'll always be here somewhere
for the day you return.

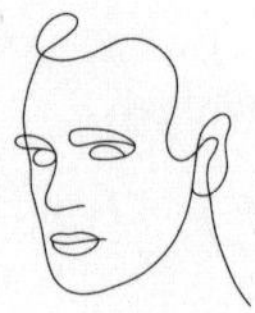

A Man Dies Twice

a man dies two deaths
one when his heart stops
and the other when his purpose is lost
the first one is easy
his mom held his hand
and his dad just had to learn
to have a drink alone one night
the other one is slow,
a cruel torture
painfully true
one day, all black they wore
the other day their tongues were bare
and all he'd become was gravestone
the world forgets who he was,
time and tide wait for none
they'd said
he was a kid back then,
didn't know how much that meant
a man dies two deaths
one where his heart looses its air
and the second when the rest of the air loses his name

two deaths,
a father, a son, a brother
two deaths but to all, the same
he's a man of two deaths
a linger of scent, a forgotten warmth, a solemn speech
one man of two deaths,
many men to come and go
and yet i stand here
i look at him
and don't really understand
which death he'd choose.

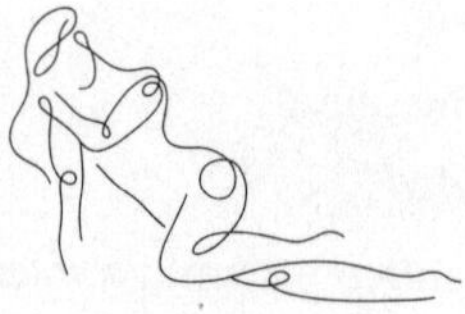

I Could Think of a Hundred Ways

i could think of a hundred ways
death would feel like
slowly tangling my bones
drying my blood
and cursing me to freeze alone
the cold embrace
of my inevitable fate
as it slowly encapsulates my being
as i am left to turn to nothing
i could imagine death
as going to high on a swing
as the breeze rushes past your cheeks
i could feel this is what would death would be
god whispers, "come on home"
and i feel the swing going high once more
i could imagine death
as the drying of flowers
ever so slowly, ever so gracefully
and as the last petals wither,
wrenched of their nectar covered blood
i could imagine death would feel like the fading of flowers

i could imagine death
as my father's embrace
warm and safe
i could imagine death painless,
like arms of love that bring me home
death could feel like all the life i could hold
i could imagine death
as my lover's eyes
a single tear drop that flushes
his skin like the warmth of guilt and anger burn his browns
and i could imagine death as the piercing sound
of silence and cries
i could imagine death as
the kisses my mother plants on my face
soft, serene;
i could imagine death as a mother
calling her child
to come rest with her
and when death finally knocks at my door
i'll look for the small moments of life in my death
and forever, will i think
there were a hundred ways i could imagine death.

In the Backseat of Your Mind

someday you will meet somebody else, and of course you will. but the existence of a newfound love won't water down the memory of us, now will it? you will give us a quiet place somewhere deep in your mind, behind all those thoughts you've never spoken out loud, with all the childhood memories, with all parts of you, you've never shown. you will hear us dancing to the sound of your old laugh and someday, you will meet her and you will tell us to quiet down. although we won't leave your memory, but we will sit and marvel at the beautiful bride and i won't wish it was me anymore. we will sit in the corners of your mind, wait for occasional moments when you'll call us out. when your son has his first heartbreak or when you'll allow yourself to see me in the eyes of your future daughter as she sobs in your arms.

you will tell them, loss is good. loss is proof there was love. you will tell them how sometimes, loving someone is simply not enough. that the end of something doesn't have to be wasted time, that is was just complete. and i will think of you, too. when i hear our song play on the radio, i'll hold the hand of the man i met after you. i'll let you out of the backseat of my own mind, occasionally to laugh about how foolish i was to be hurt about you finding someone new. you will think about me and as will i, we'd be contempt with each other's loss. we'd still be sitting in the backseat of our own minds, hope the others we find would make us happier than we tried making each other and we'll be okay with finding other people and never seeing each other again except for the slow dancing in our minds, because that meant there was real love. and i'd be grateful. how i'd be so. damn. grateful.

You Asked Me if I Loved You

you asked me if i loved you
oh but you don't see it
the way i'd burn
in the pits of hell to keep you warm
through the gates of heaven
drown in your sin
till i am covered in this passion
you don't see it, do you?
i'd rip my heart open
if you asked me to
break my bones
and build you a home
shield you from the moonlight
as i hold the burning stars
in my bare palms
only if you asked
how, i'd burn for you
but you don't see it, do you?
i'd push the pen
through my skin
if you lived between these words i carve

syllables that'll only ever know your name
stand between the embers
only ever yours, forever undone
and pray for forever
rip the sky in two
for us two,
you asked me if i loved you
you don't see it, do you?

A Lover, a Beggar, a Woman

something so feminine
something so feminine in me
i'll sit across from you
rip open my chest to give you a heart that beats
bones and ribs and all that you could need
blood of warmth and all that only calls your name
something so feminine in me
to make a cage of my own bones
stranded and alone
something so feminine
a lover, a beggar, a woman
a lonely home
walls of whispers, walls of stone
something ever so feminine
delicate and dainty
a woman's love is only worthy
if needed by the man
a lover, a beggar, a damsel
feminine and true
a palette of black and blue
a fire to my cage

a shackle to my rage
a damsel that must be saved
something so feminine
beautiful and broken
serene and solemn
adam and a woman
and a cage of bones
what you could call your own
something so feminine
and someone so alone

No Flowers Please

no flowers please
when you're at my grave
and how ever solemn or damp it may be,
no flowers, not today please
take the flowers home
and plant them in all the places
i felt alive
plant one in your heart
and one in my garden
and grow and learn
from all i lived and all i couldn't
and come to see me often
but no flowers please
take the flowers back and give them to the girl with the aching heart
for she still has air in her lungs
and give them to the boy who's somebody's son
to a heart that's been broken
more than once
my grave, come see me
come and stay
stay and bleed

but no flowers please
not today, not here
for i don't want you
to honor the place i lay dead
honor every place i lived
my lungs held words,
my breath held thoughts i never said
but don't honor where i stay
ever so quiet ever so thoughtless
bring grace everywhere
my heart beat
because death isn't worth
if life wasn't lived
no flowers, none please.

If I Had Nine Lives

if i had nine lives
i'd spend the first two by the coast
learn to swim and learn to drown
and as the water sets into my lungs
and the last breath of air turns to stone
i'll think of the next seven lives i have to spend
if i had nine lives
i'd spend two with each of my parents
grow in their shadow and learn their flaws
and i'll hold the only hand
that brought me here
as i trace the lines of fate
that binds us
if i had nine lives
i'd spend the next alone
solitude and confinement
one of my own bones
and when the insanity and loneliness get to me
i'll perish with all but four more lives to live
if i had nine lives
i'd spend one being like my father

embody his ways and fate
and when death knocks at my door
i'll trust the only fate i've ever known
if i had nine lives
i'd spend the next living the ideal life
i'd spend it exactly like my mom would say
married by thirty and a casket by seventy
if i had nine lives
i'd spend one waiting
waiting on love and waiting for you
they say insanity grows where love waters it
and i'd water my insanity
to wait for you at grocery stores and bus stands
and when no one comes
i'll hold death's hand
if only i had nine lives
i'd find you this time
learn you and make you mine
nine lives would be worth it for you
but i don't have nine lives
i've only this one
so i'll spend this searching
searching for you in strangers and empty skies
and when i finally meet you
maybe all this will be worth the while

Devil's Daughter

but i burn
and up in flames,
there, the smoke calls my name
and i run,
right into the pit of fire
because he calls me home,
my father
i am the devil's daughter
i look in the mirror and i see him
looking over my shoulder
i am the monster
i was warned about
and you can run to a lot of places
when what you're running from
is not yourself.
so do i burn now?
i am set on fire, do i perish?
it's not hell if i can see her
through the reflection,
and she's beautiful, still.

she wears my eyes and hair
and sits so calm
she's across the mirror,
she sees me burn
and she feels my fire in her
her palms, soft as feathers
and mine, harsh as the words i mutter
do you see who i am, father?
i am your daughter.
you are the tempest
and me?
i am the devil's own creation.

A Man's Love

in the damsels eyes
the very that seek love
but love, she believes is not worth
if not by a man
the damsel is distressed
starved of the love of a man
through bones, through lungs
through my very own thoughts
the damsels, can't you see needs love
a love, enough to protect, enough to hold
enough to keep, enough to mold
mold her to a woman
for a girl is only a woman if loved by a man
the hollow of the masculine palm
where she rests hers
only there she feels worth sinking in to her skin
a man's love
the damsel, the woman
starve and sob
for the man's love.

Two Hearts on the Floor

two hearts on the floor
one is mine
both are yours
one beats for the hope of it all
another grows tired and hurt
from all the hope of all that's lost
two hearts on the floor
one is mine and both are yours
one that beats for the sake of the other
one that's on death's door
and that heart's not mine anymore
two hearts on the floor
sit down and stitch together
veins and words and whispers galore
don't stop beating just yet
too much to live and love and hope
two hearts on the floor
one is mine and both are yours.

Bests

the best music
the best memories
the best places
and in all those bests
you were better
i showed you what i loved
because well, i loved you more
now you're gone
and selfishly enough
you have taken my bests with you
now i only have
music, memories, places
you took the bests away.
you took the bests away.

Loving Someone is Never a Waste

loving someone is never a waste because loving someone is proof that you're so full of it, you're so full of love. loving someone, can never be a waste because all the love we bring with us is all that we take back and all that we leave behind. god sends us with love to spread it, to live it and to be it. loving someone is never a waste because if all our hearts bleed, then god sent us with band-aids as love. if all our hearts seem to break, god sent us with the strength to fix what's been broken, if the world always feels so cruel, god sent us with faith to see right.

and if someday, the love that you give happens to not be the love you get back, always remember, loving someone is never a waste.

The Girl Sits Down at the Table

the girl sits down at the table
"i forgave you a million times
over and over again
and i will still choose to do it today
because that's how much i love you."
the boy settles in his chair
he meets her eyes and somewhere
between words and tears
he says
"no my dear
that's not how much you love me
that's how much you don't love yourself."
the girl is taken aback
and with the same crack
in her voice she says
"i loved you enough to stay,
you loved me enough to let me go"
the boy reaches out his hand
to hold hers
their palms sink in to the hollow
of one another

and he says
“you loved me enough to stay
and i loved myself enough to know
that i could let you go.
you couldn’t let me go
because you never loved yourself
not enough to know you needed better”
“but what if i wanted you to be better?”
and her tears never felt so heavy
the boy lets go of her palm
and ever so slowly
“you didn’t want me to be better.
you wanted yourself to forget you deserved better.”

I Bleed Therefore I Am

i bleed therefore i am
because it takes your pain
to prove that you're alive
the blood in your veins
and air in your lungs
the words you've never said
and all the times you felt as one
and i bleed therefore i am
because if there's no blood on my palms
how can i say there's blood in my heart
the blood it pumps
to the moon and back
i bleed therefore i am
bleed as a whole, bleed and i broke
i bleed because i am human
and i will bleed till i cannot heal
because all hearts need to be broken
give it two minutes, give it twenty
i bleed therefore i am
give me sanity
and i do not hide the blood i loose

because the blood that flows
is the blood that proves
proves that i breathe
proves i am me
and i bleed, bleed and bleed
today and tomorrow
i bleed therefore i am
and i bleed till i am hollow.

Spare Me a Minute

spare me a minute
i'll tell you about every time i told you
i loved you
how much i meant it
spare me two,
i'll finally find the courage to
to hand you
all the letters that never
made it past my diary
spare me three
and i could finally
come lay in your arms
for all the time that i've got
with me
spare me four
and i could tell you i miss you
i want you to come home
and you could kiss me on the forehead
pull me in and hug me tight
i could beg a bit
you'd spare me five

five minutes pass too soon
i never got to hold you
but you say you could spare me six
and i fall to your feet
"thank you" i'd say,
and you'd wipe my face of all the tears i've shed
next time you'd save me seven,
i'd hope and think about all i could tell you
seven whole minutes of your time
seven minutes etched in my veins seven minutes in my mind
and what if you could spare me eight?
eight minutes too long, you'd say
i'll cry, you'd cave
eight minutes i'd get
tell you all about what the world did to me
you would hold me, and in those eight minutes
i'd fall apart,
you'd put me back together
eight minutes too short
you'd take nine to put me back together
nine minutes, i'd hope and pray for nine lives
next to you, and nine minutes fly by
you could save me ten
but ten minutes you couldn't lend
so i'd sit on my floor
you walk away, close my door
and tears, they'll dry
i say i'll be fine
be grateful you spared me one
be somber, for you could spare none.

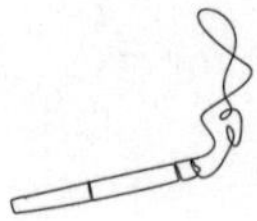

Half-Burnt Cigar

do you hear my voice over the smoke?
the smoke you light
to run from the sight
of the world burning
yours, and mine
and do you see through the smoke?
the smoke you try to blind
your own eyes with
so you can't tell what died
yours, and mine
and do you reach out into the smoke
the smoke of your half-burnt cigar
the cigar you lit
from the very flames you put in my heart
smoke of red and tears
and your half-burnt cigar
rips me apart, smoke and paper
and yet you'd have the half-burnt cigar
than my hands
in your palm, smoke and paper,
and a broken heart.

Two Things I Feel

two things i feel,
two ways i break,
two things i'll never say,
two times i stayed,
two words i hold back,
two halves of me too far away
two tears i cry
and two that i dry
two ways i pull together all i kept
two minutes too soon
you broke me in two,
the two halves i don't get.

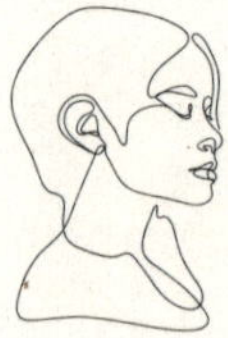

Life Lessons

life lessons you were too young to know

⊙ there is a big difference between fighting for someone you love and fighting for someone to love you. a love that's always only hoped for, fought for, longed for but never gotten, does not exist.

⊙ there is another huge difference between letting go of something and ignoring its existence. you can bury things that haven't died yet and it doesn't kill them, it simply makes them haunt you.

⊙ nothing changes, if nothing changes. life is worth living only if you make it. no one else gets to teach you how to lead life.

⊙ keep what you can love and let the rest go. it will be hard, but for everything and everyone that you cannot bring yourself to love, there's something and someone willing to.

⊙ healing doesn't always look like clear skin, aesthetic journals or a smiling face, sometimes, it's the damp pillow case and the smudged mascara but the guts to still smile in the mirror.

⊙ no one taught you that there is silence in every absence but not every silence is going to be absence, love isn't always so loud. often, it is the silence that lets us hear the love.

What If I Don't Feel Like Being a Good Person Today?

you came down to my house the other day and cried in my lap. you whispered through tears,
"what if i don't feel like being a good person today?" and a few minutes later, another tear hit your cheek. it wasn't yours, it was mine. and i held you tight because i hate the thought that no one taught you that it's okay not to be the bigger person most days. when we were little, mom used to tell you, "always be the bigger person dove, be kind and love everyone." no one taught you that hate is justified. you learned that with time, hate and anger die. that's what they said, right? the thing is, there's a very fine line between dying and getting buried. you thought, if you could keep on piling love on top of all that hate, it would make the love real and the hate die. few drinks later, when the love begins to fade, hate wakes from the dead and tells you that it never died because you never felt it. the way to kill hate (i know kill is a strong word) is not to bury it. you can bury things alive and that's why it still hurts. you need to feel the hate and anger to kill it. so dove, when you asked me, "what if i don't feel like being like a good person today?" i'd be grateful and somber. grateful you had the courage to feel the hate today, somber you felt too weak to feel it before.

And That's the Blood It Costs

and that's the blood it costs
for me to prove that i'm dying
three cuts to thirteen
minutes drenched in red
and my wound bleeds
because that's what it takes
for the wounds in my head
to be wounds they'd care about
and all that flows red
is all that begs
for a life that's lost
and all that's never heard
is all that you needed to know
because i wonder
and i truly do
i'm dying on the inside
but at what cost?

Privilege

"at least she's got someone to talk to. i don't even have that. all i have
is myself."
that's what you said, you cried in my arms because you wanted to be
heard so bad. i held you tighter to my chest as you sobbed and wept.
"i cry, i sob and i rot. all by myself. all i'll ever have is myself" and
if in that moment i could do anything other than hold you as you
fell, i would've told you that it is a privilege. we're all here only for
ourselves. you never needed anyone else, and that's what you find
so hard to believe. you cry, you sob and you rot. but the next day
you get up, you hurt and you wipe your damn tears. on your own
and if only i could've told you that's a privilege. it's a privilege to be
the only one with yourself. it's a privilege to know yourself and it's
a privilege to wipe your own tears. you don't see it now, but when
you're sixty, you'd be grateful your fourteen-year-old self was strong
enough to wipe her own tears. wept and cried but she got up. she got
up. on her own.
all you'll ever have is yourself. and for all that it's worth, that's a
privilege.

Pressed Flowers

pressed flowers
five roses of white
and four of pink
pressed flowers in the pages
of my diary
pressed against pages of ink
ink, that draws both you and me
one fine line that tugs at you
another, i pull
pressed flowers in pages of my diary
pressed into stains on my writing
pressed as stains on my soul
five roses of white
and four of pink
and i bleed with the ink
that i tie around us
pulling in tight
pressed flowers in my diary
pressed against whispers of longing
for you to be mine.

What Is Love

"love is passion and passion is insane. maybe, that's what it is,
it's love that's insane."
one friend says,
"what is love if not insane? what is love if it doesn't wrench your guts?"
the other fiddles with the glass of wine in his hand,
the other second, turns to face a frame of his wife and says,
"it's called peace."
the friend gets up and sits at the feet of the chair,
"love is supposed to be calm and quiet and safe. insanity is bullshit.
love is peace."
and it's funny
because i'd actually agree with both
but the other friend says
"if you're not insane for love
there is no passion
love needs passion."
i chuckled a slight bit,
enough for them both to look to me
and i looked at them with a grin, as i admit
the married friend sets his glass of wine

on the table, sits beside his friend
"i find peace in my love.
i don't need passion.
is my love not real?"
and i'll look at the half empty bottle of wine
on the marble floor
true love never needed alcohol to justify it anyway, passion, let alone.
i'm on the bed,
i'll smile and i'll say
"i think it's foolish
how you subject love to words
'love needs passion'
and you need to be taught what love is,"
"what do you think love is then?"
my friend says.
ah, "love"
"how foolish of you,
to look for the meaning of love.
to think love needs passion
oh how foolish of you
to wonder if a love
without the need of passion
is real
and how foolish of me
to think you'll ever know
what love means."

Believe in Love

"believe in love, only because you're so full of it"

you told me the other day, "i don't really believe in love anymore" and well, all i could do was think to myself how someone so full of it, refused to believe love is truly real. a few cups of coffee later, i sat on my balcony alone and it really hit me. why you did not think love was real. my dear, you've got the idea of love all wrong.

love was not the boy who left you all alone, love was you getting up the next day, still. love was not your middle school friend group that made you feel like you were not enough, love was you having the courage to unlearn all of their hatred. love was not the family who couldn't support you, love was you having the guts to support yourself. love was not some random man telling you that you were beautiful, love was you believing you were anyway. love is not all that you have lost and all that you cannot get. love is all that you are.

it hurts me to think that you do not know what love is. my little dove, it hurts me to think you believe in love only because you thought someone else would give it to you.

that's the thing about love, you don't believe in love because they said that they loved you. you believe in it because you had the courage to love them back.

Save Your Breath

save your breath, for you might need it
to tell me you still love me
hush, as i push the hair
away from your face
behind your ear
save your breath
for you may need it
when you decide to speak again
come and lay in my lap
tell me about how the world's so cruel
but don't say too much,
save your breath
you might need it again
this time,
tell me the world would be better
if things were different
hush, as you sob in this despair
of guilt, words that shackle your throat
my love, won't you save your breath
you might need it
screaming, trying to come back home.

I Am My Own Grave

i am my own grave
stone-cold and damp
from all the tears i've cried
and all these poems i write
in the shine of a barely lit lamp
shallow and narrow
only till these shatters of me
would fit
frozen in the shackles of time
lips of a lost life
as i utter words of disgrace
i am my own grave
dead, from all the life i lived
and from all that i haven't
one breath, i take
rest fly by
i am my own grave,
stone-cold and damp
leaves dry and flowers fade
lord, i'm my own grave.

It's Been 15 Pages

you've walked in a room
first thing you see
crumpled pages and you'd not believe
i'd actually be gone
you'd run your fingers over my diary
long gone dusty
15 pages left empty
and you'd question
in what universe i'd leave pages empty
so you sit in my chair
you take in the scent in the air
15 pages left and the rest pass by
like all those nights
laughing till the crack of daylight
and your eyes fill with tears
run your fingers
over words you read, echoes you hear
"15 pages left and i'll see you when we meet one last time
hold on to my words all this while
because 15 pages pass by and next time
you could say it's been 15 pages since you were mine."

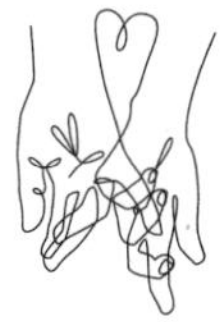

It's Been 15 Pages (Part 2)

fifteen pages of my diary
under cold swept doubts and dust
and scent of scandal in the air
it makes you miss me
so you sit in my chair
feel me on your skin
and deep in your bones
run your fingers over words i've carved
moments we've owned
and fifteen pages
they fly by
so you put the diary aside
chuckle inside your mind
maybe next time
i'd leave fifteen pages empty
and you could say it's been
fifteen pages since you were mine

I Wonder If You'll Grieve Me

i wonder if you grieve me
if you ever sit alone
and think of me
when you wake up
to no calls or texts
i wonder if your heart
it feels hollow
an empty void
sinking in your chest
a pill too hard to swallow
i wonder if you see me
out in a restaurant
and you see me
i wonder if you feel anxious
or if your bones tangle
with veins of blood
that runs cold
dying to come home
to a soul
who's not yours to hold.

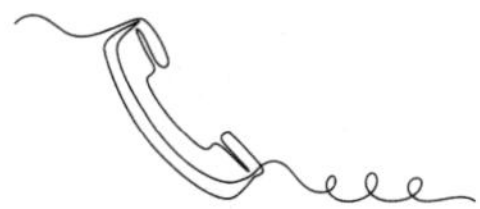

I Called You Tonight

i called you tonight
but you didn't answer
it rung 3 times
and i cut the call
i've gotten used to this new usual
i'll text and you won't reply
i'll call and it'll only ever ring
3 times.
i don't really remember
when us became you and me
and when the phone lines gathered rust
and when all we ever were had turned to dust
but i do remember that your phone rung thrice
it only ever rang thrice

Seven Days, Twenty-Four Hours (Part 2)

when we talk hours,
six you slept
woke up and cried
you didn't like what you dreamt
three you spent
glancing over picture frames
old and dusty
and the tenderness in my smile
makes you miss me
two you spent in the shower
head in your hands,
the way shit always ends
and you walk out, your skin burns
is it me or is it the water?
you really can't tell, but damn it hurts.
one you spent with your dog
and i wonder if you thought
about me in the halls when your voice
it echoed, did you hear me come in through the back door?
that's twelve hours you waste
because of a love you'll never taste

and the rest twelve
you spend
in the prison of your mind
and i know, the mind it's never kind
i wonder if your skin stings
was it the shower? or was it me?
that's twelve hours you spend
in this small cell, we are all one
i'm a prisoner right next to you
and that's twenty-four hours we waste
in search of each other
we were next to all this late.

Clever Poetry

i wonder how many times
a poem i write
messes with your head
the small words, size of an ant
pinch at your skin and sulk with your guilt
how many times would you have smelt the roses you'd get
in the air of your room,
long, they'd been dead
but i wonder, i truly do
does it mess with you?
the clever poetry,
i know how to make you sad
so do you really stain your palms
with tears you cry
you taste one and what does it feel like
guilt? fear? reminiscence?
and i wonder how many times
clever words, they tug at your skin
and take you back and make you relive us
i wonder and i truly do.
do my words get you stuck?

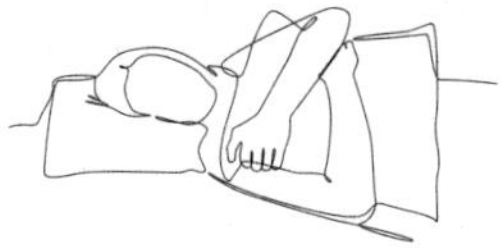

They Say

they say
it's one breath you take
between life and death
and i wonder
if in those 2 seconds of time
you'll think of me
will my voice ring in your ear?
will my laugh put you to sleep again?
will you smile at the thought
of having me hold you
one last time?
take you back to March
when all you were was a young boy
with a heavy heart
and too much to carry?
and you remind yourself
that my touch has been etched
into all those parts you were so scared to show
tell me if it's one breath you'll take,
will you think of me
before you go?

They Were Summer Nights

they were summer nights
early July
and late at night
do you remember what you whispered
over the phone,
your voice echoed
in my empty room
i drew those words,
fine into paper
50 crumpled pages
all over my cold floor
and i could've sworn
you had known.
"i loved you yesterday
full moon night
and i'll love you today
there's no moon in sight,
i loved you last month,
it had rained
and i love you this one,
the only rain i saw was on your cheeks,

i loved you under a sky with all our answers
and i love you today
with none,
hidden behind clouds and whispers
i love you,
today. yesterday. and tommorow."

Cry

"you look just like me when you cry
please stop crying"
my mother's voice would stumble in my ear
is me looking like her when i cry
her biggest fear?
"no my dear,
i want you to look like me when you smile"
and i can look in her eyes
the feeling of knowing
that when i fall,
broken feet and broken bones
mother,
you fear i look like you
when i cry
because you fear
that when i fall
i fall into a path you seem to know.

Missing Rib

and god made us for each other
i will whisper
they won't believe me
and i will tell them
i'm his missing rib,
he needs me
and so to convince them,
to convince myself
i'll sit for hours
and carve my bones
to be loved,
to be a rib,
his rib, the missing rib
and Eve;
she looks at me
disappointment floods her eyes
her dear child,
till all i become
is truly a rib,
not his rib
but only a bone,

lost life, and my mother.
i'd say, i was his missing rib
why won't they believe me?
my mother looks
to her daughter,
i claw at dirt,
despair in her eyes,
her star child burnt.

My Father's Daughter

"she has her father's eyes"
and i read a quote once
a girl either grows into a woman
or her father
so i look deep
and set my gaze far into the mirror
all i'll ever see is my father
it's not the brown eyes we share
it's not hair
that falls down to my shoulders
or the face that makes us both
look a little more similar
i looked and i looked and i wished
that if only limited to hair and face
i would grow into a woman,
perhaps my mother
but i see
and i spy with my father's blessed eye
claw marks as we share,
tears of innocence fall and
we clench on to despair

fifty crumpled pages
all over our bedroom floor
and i know you had better known
i am my father's daughter
we sink into one another
and i tilt over my window pane
push the hair we share
behind my ear
father, i'm all your mistakes
all over again.

Things You Outgrew

it's 2015, rainy day in June and you're in your mum's backseat listening to the sound of the raindrops against the window. it's a normal saturday, you're with dad and a math problem, the news playing in the background. it's a sunny evening in the garden with your childhood friends and you're laughing. the same laughs that echo in your head at midnight. now, you're 15 and you sit alone in a taxi, it's not as fun anymore. you're 15 and solve your own math problems and somehow it's worse. you're 15 and don't go out with your childhood friends to play and you miss being in company of silly jokes. it's the same hollow feeling you get when that sweater from 2022 doesn't fit you anymore and when you realized they stopped making those raspberry candies.

sometimes, whether it's a sweater that was way too short for you to begin with or your dad unable to explain a math sum to you, you miss it. and even more times, it's never about what you outgrew but more about what you were like when you outgrew those things.

Cobblestone Streets

cobblestone streets
and i wonder if you think of me,
your feet press against the ground
and the sound
of the rain on the cold road
i wonder if you look into windows
of homes
and ache to see me
dancing around the kitchen
with my hair undone
and i wonder if you ever see someone
with the same eyes as me
and you look as deep as you can
try to find all the answers
and clues
and a map to a road that leads you
back home and i wonder if you think about me
when the radio turns on
and the sky turns grey
but music won't drown your guilt
and that half empty cup

won't justify us
and you're walking home
on broken cobblestones
and you see me
and i wonder if you think
about us,
somewhere initials carved
on broken bones and empty photos
i really hope you think about me.

Bring an Umbrella

let the mascara run down when he makes you cry and wipe those tears with your own hands. the boy who sits across from you is not the love of your life and the boy on the football team is not the end of the world. you're a growing human and you'll make mistakes, don't try to cover them up. wear the loud boots and the skirt because no one will remember what you wear on a random tuesday, and be friendly. make friends and be kind because the love you give is all you leave behind and all you take with you. don't be mean to the girl in the mirror, at 60 years old, she's going to be the only person there for you and the only person in your casket.

eat your mum's home-cooked food because you'll miss it one day. allow yourself to be sad and happy and angry and hurt and all those emotions you think you're weak for showing. let it bleed. let the pillow grow damp and your voice become coarse because one day, it will get better. don't let the girl in middle school tell you you're good for nothing and don't let your first boyfriend convince you that your worth is defined by him. don't feel embarrassed when you repeat an outfit, it's just as cute as the first time, and don't yell at your mum. she's a true and best friend.

go out with your friends instead of dates with boys because 5-6 years later you'll be in different cities. you're not "run through" because your ex-boyfriend was too insecure and you're definitely not worthless because the kids at school who don't know past your name said so. listen to your older sister when she tells you to not go out with that boy and come home and cry in her arms when he breaks your heart.

your dad is the only man who'll ever love you right and your brother is annoying but he's going to be the first one to be banging at that boy's doorstep when he makes you cry. find true female friends and never hurt another girl. dance in the rain and sing in the sunlight. smell flowers and pet dogs, wave at strangers and tell the new girl she's pretty. be kind. be loveable. be happy. and when it rains, bring an umbrella.

Gaze's Slave

but i am yet another slave
to your gaze
and as i set in front of you
i am a little girl
dancing around the room
for your attention
hoping and craving and wishing to be
heard and seen and noticed
but every time you step further
my hand clutches tighter
and i don't complain of your negligence
because beggars can't be choosers
and as you lift your gaze even slightly from me
i collapse and shatter
because i am a slave
and if only the little girl
in me would stop dancing
accept that she's just another thought
and you don't actually love her
but beggars aren't choosers
and i can't choose to not love you.

Cinematic Heartbreak

but they liked my sadness somber and held under
and they liked my tears only till they were a performance
i was good with words
but good enough only to be applauded for never being taken seriously
my voice grew quieter as they told me
they liked my sadness
my mind never really went quiet after that
taken aback
my world became me thinking
that if they wrench me off my words and my blood
i'd be drunk on my own tears
and i stayed low and quiet
hanging on to whatever i could stitch
out of broken parts of me
they seemed to admire
till only i never cut them with the shard of broken glass that was my skin
because they liked my sadness only till it was a performance
and they liked my shrieks only till i could sing after they liked my
tears only till they could drink it later
and so i never showed sadness as an emotion i performed every time
i cried thirsty of my own feelings i never shrieked again
and that's how a poet i became.

Would You Have Known

and if one day
you decided to sit down
and read every poem i've ever written
if you decided to run your fingers over
words i've carved on paper
would you feel the paper as your skin
would you see my words replicate your eyes
would you see your voice
drawn into the way my hand writes
would you see your face in every word and syllable i ever wrote
and if you decided one day
to read every poem i ever told
would you be surprised?
or would you have known?

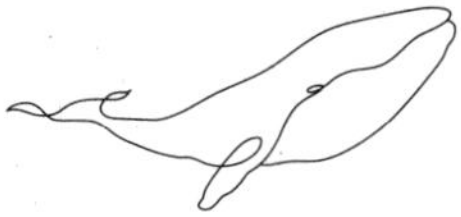

Veins of Hate

hate was woven into her bones
thorns punctured into supple skin
of infinitude and innocence
tears turn to stones
she holds her knife dear and close
for it's the only affection she's known
holds it to her throat,
till it pierces through her neck
words she never said as blood, that pours
runs to her palms
palms that never held petals
grow rough from thorns
lips of life grow weak from their strained smile
and a soul that never carried love,
dust, as she becomes, all she asks
"come and lay me
in petals and flowers
do not wake me for if it is death i have to choose
to be mourned and loved once more
it is death i will choose but
when i lay promise me, you will love me."

His Tears Seep into My Skin

his tears seep into my skin
bury in my bones
his sadness will puncture into my lungs
i'll exhale and inhale with holes
from his words
that i carry
my spine will twist and break
from the weight
of burdens i don't own
but i'll carry his sadness
in my bones
in my throat
in my eyes
and in my home
i'll hold his tears for him
in everything i'll write
i'll stain my pages and pillows
and when my heart and snew
break and fall softly
i'll take his somber to my grave
i'll bury it beside me.

Men Don't Cry

"men don't cry"
oh but they do.
they weep and sob and scream
a lady far smarter hears his sobs
from behind the words he'll say
she'll see his tears from behind
the smile that's trying so hard to hide
she'll see the water roll down his cheeks
from the crinkle of his eye
and she'll hold him
and words and tears he'll cry
"men won't sob, men aren't weak"
but the screams
that punch his head
won't dull his voice
and the rains he'll cry
won't dim his sunshine
and only a lady
far wiser will know better
than to say
"men. don't. cry."

Maybe 20 Years Later

maybe 20 years later
when i'm at the grocery store
i'll find you again
you'll have oranges in your cart
and i'll have apples in mine
and you'll look at me
and i'll look at you
and for a moment, my bones will tangle
we'll talk over words and feelings hushed
i'll never say, but you'll have heard
i'll tell you i got the house
with the white gate
like we always talked about
except my halls have never felt more empty
i'll tell you i hung photos of the flowers
you'd get me
you'll smile
and all this,
will be worth the while
you'll tell me about your life
you'll be settled overseas

soaring through the skies
and how all you'll ever see
in those beautiful blues
is me
you'll tell me how the sky
reminds you of my nail paint
and i'll laugh
as my thoughts grow faint
my phone will ring
the apples in my cart will toss
the oranges in yours remain still
and as i'll tell you
i better get going
you'll tell me you're proud of me
and i'll say "likewise"
it's funny
with time, how you seem to forget,
how some things felt so meant to be
you'll feel the emptiness
you've been trying to fill
with portraits of flowers
and blue nail paint
and it will sink
into your bones and words
so the next time
when i go to a grocery store
i'll hope to find you in the aisles
and when i don't find you,
i think i'll pick up some oranges this time.

I'll Wait

i'll sit here tangled in my own bones
i'll wait for it to pass
hold my breath
and hold my words
take to death
and when i lay
i'll only wish for you
to come and cry
on my grave
flowers will bloom from the tears you'll cry
and i'll rest
and i'll die.

Once Every Year

once every year
and when the clock strikes midnight
i'll sit down on my floor
open the same old box of photos
i hadn't opened before
this once every year,
stained cheeks
writing till my fingers bleed
i'll sit in my chair and stare
into emptiness and ghosts of your shadows
this once every year,
my ears will ring of echoes
i can't push out
and hide somewhere while these thoughts
get loud
and this once every year,
i'll think of you,
i know you'll think of me
and what we were supposed to be.

I Look in People's Windows

i look in people's windows
hoping i'd see us
dancing around the kitchen
in the refrigerator light
just one more time
maybe us in another universe
where we are working out
i look in people's windows
in case that's us

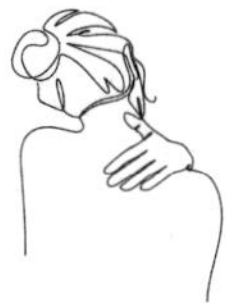

And When You Cup Her Face

and when you cup her face
between your palms
i wonder if she knows
they were the same that ripped me apart
and when you look at me
do you see my hollow
longing for the one thing
you so relentlessly stole,
my love,
i know love exists
because i was full of it
and i gave it all to you
just for you to bury it in someone else
and i hope that when she sleeps in your arms
she knows it isn't you she's fallen in love with
it's me
and i'm the woman in the shadow
lonely and somber
for a love
i couldn't keep for longer.

Watch

watch as the poet
sits and paints
his deepest wounds
into artwork you admire
watch his fingers burn
from the fire
he lights for his work to shine
watch as he drinks his own tears
so he's always somber
they said no one knows a poet
better than his sadness
and so he turns every cry
into art and
engraves every last word
onto his skin
and as the last breath
had left his lungs
there was a portrait
of all his cries for help
on a wall,
so beautifully hung

Scare

it began to scare you,
didn't it?
the reflection in the mirror
because every monster
you ever feared
stood right across from you
every monster you ever ran from
is every monster you became
because everything you ran from
is everything you once loved.

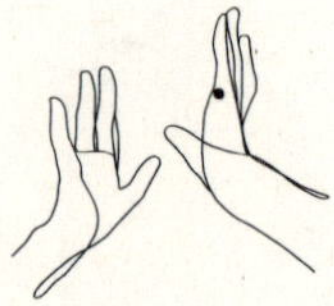

And When You Were Five

and when you are five, the world makes less sense to you, why the big kids cry over their phone or why your mom prefers wearing makeup or why your older sister is scared to walk home alone. you think to yourself, maybe when you are older, the world will seem more understandable, more reasonable and you'll understand all the things that confused you at five but now, you are fifteen, the world makes even less sense to you. you know more than what you knew at five, you know why the older kids cried with their phones in their hands, your mom wearing makeup, your older sister not wanting to walk home alone but the world still scares you, and at fifteen, when you sit alone in your taxi, raindrops on the window, you realize the world made more sense at five.

You Are in Every Word She Says

you are in every word she says
every poem she writes
every time she smiles
she owns the body
but you own the mind
you occupy each thought
and behind each phrase that leaves her lips
she whispers your name with
and as desperately as she wishes
they would be oblivious
to her obvious
fascination
it is hard to hide
behind eyes in love.

Faces in the Street

faces in the street
they say
every person has a story to tell
every pair of eyes speak a new language
but as i walk
faces in the street
i desperately glare at them
hoping to hear their stories
understand their eyes
but all my efforts die
ashes and cries
faces in the street
and i wish i could see them too
but when i walk alone
faces in the street
all i'll ever see
is you.

Last Time

last time
one last time
i held you
selfishly tried to keep you
but you're like sand
in my bare hand
slipping away no matter how tight i grasp
one last time
i hoped you would stay
but you wouldn't wait another minute
one last time.
and then, i hoped a hundred times again

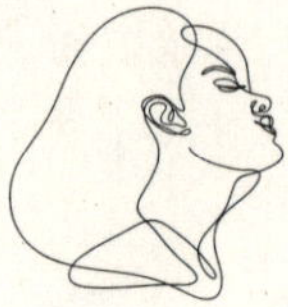

Yours

in your absence
that i drown in these days
i've learned to hold onto small
parts of you
that you left behind
music, interests, even your name
i hold onto small parts of you
so maybe one day
i can find enough of "yours"
to make a "you"

Maybe

and maybe you were right mom.
maybe i should have held onto your fingers
for a minute longer
because i can't walk straight anymore
and maybe
i should have looked in your eyes
instead of looking at the mirror
because in your eyes
is the only reflection i seem to like
and maybe
i should have stayed closer to you so i didn't get lost
because i can't find my way home now
and if only i had noticed how you
handled all the strife
today i'd also know how
and you were right mom.
if only 7-year-old me had stayed in your arms on nights she was cold
she'd feel warmer at 14 years old
and maybe you were right mom
because in all these years
you were my only true friend all along.

Write a Poem About Me!

"write a poem about me!"
you say,
and i know you
meant it sarcastically,
but i laugh a little too
because dear god,
only if you knew.
my notebook and paper and pen
and thoughts
only ever call out your name
and as desperately as i hold my ink
wishing for it to write anything other
than your name
it fixes itself,
set on writing only the words
that make your sound
and as desperately as i rip pages
out my notebook
hoping to craft something
other than you, all it takes is a smile
for another poem about you.

Where Do All the Words in My Head Go?

where do all the words in my head go?
words that never made it to paper
thoughts i kept from their ears
to hear
where do all my broken thoughts go?
strands and lingering loose ends
never tied
in lines of word craft
thoughts and quotes
that die unnoted
ghosts of words my lips never said
stay in any head
become the echoes that scratch my mind
because i never fully understood
where do all my unsaid thoughts go?
who do they hide behind?

Poem

i've never quite written love poetry
for you
because, yes, i could sit here
draw comparisons to every flower in my garden
every rain i've ever soaked in
every wind that's brushed through my hair
every ray of sunshine my skin has felt
yes, i could draw comparison to every book in my shelf
every high of bibliosmia i've gotten
every line that's ever sat in my eyes
and never been forgotten
since
but i do not believe
any of these
could replicate even partial essence of you
i do not believe that a flower
could come close to your smile
no rain has ever completely drenched me
as your aura has
no wind has ever stroked my cheek
lifted my chin

no ray of sunshine has ever held me
quite like you did
and i could bring you back to my books
search for you in every word and line
but you're a one of a kind
and i do not think
the feeling of bibliosmia has ever gotten me as high as your eyes have
no word no sentence no quote no phrase
has ever made home to my eyes like you have
and perhaps the feeling of knowing
i'll never find you in anything
other than what i hold of you in my arms
keeps me holding on rather tighter.

Anatomy of a Goodbye

and with pain
i watch you pack your bags
with doubt
i open my doors
and question every moment we've ever owned
with relapse
i try to hold on to hands,
on coldest nights, felt warmest,
now feel foreign
but with withdrawal
i take steps back
lead you to my doors as you leave,
with reminiscence, i think about each second
of when your lips mouthed my name
in every conversation
and with a heavy heart
a few broken walls, gallons of blood we shed
veins and snew, ripped in passion
with acceptance,
i look in the reflection, you left

Nail Polish

my nail polish is chipped,
and there's a dried tear in my eye
my hair's a mess and, so are my bones
tangles that hold
words and rots and all.
my heart is slow and soft,
so soft that it goes quiet
every now and then.
there's a wilt in my rhymes,
and deaths of sounds on my tongue.
my lungs feel heavy,
and oh, i should fix my nail polish.

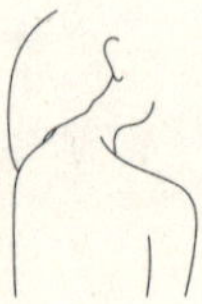

A Heart Without a Scar

a heart without a scar is a heart that's never lived. scars are beautiful signs of growth and growth is never easy. growth is tears of mascara and wet pillow cases. sad songs on repeat and closed doors but growth and healing is also the smell of fresh air and laughter. it's also a smile in the mirror and forgiveness along the way. healing is never going to be easy. healing is never going to be quick. and i think that's what makes it so very beautiful. to be with a wound but to know that when your wound becomes a scar it won't hurt anymore. so today, to all my precious people who sit with a wound today, let me remind you, "wounds change to bruises to then scars, pain changes to another flower in your garden"

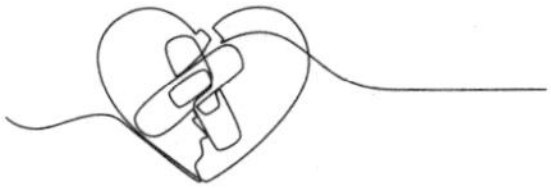

Healing

and when you're hurt,
remember that your wound
will, with time, become a bruise,
your bruise,
will, with time,
become a scar,
and well aware i stand
that scars remain
but when it rains
watch it trickle past your scar
and it won't burn
scars remain,
but the pain
with it, dies
plant a flower for the pain
inside your heart
and next time with a wound,
take a petal and remind yourself
wounds change to bruises to then scars
pain changes to another flower in your garden.

He Buys Her Flowers

he buys her flowers
but he doesn't know her favorite kind
he sits and looks at her eyes
but he doesn't know what's behind
he holds her hand
but doesn't question her scars
he kisses her
but doesn't look into her smile
he holds her when she cries
but doesn't ask why
he says he likes her voice
but doesn't hear her words
he looks at her
but doesn't look to her
and when she leaves
he blames himself
for not knowing
how to love her

Something So Feminine

something so feminine wearing mascara
and something so feminine watching it drip down my cheeks
something so feminine keeping my mouth shut
something so feminine knowing words cut deeper than knives
something so feminine holding together
broken shackles around my wrists
something so feminine wanting to fall apart
something so feminine looking at the stars
something so feminine not knowing where you are
something so feminine clutching him close
something so feminine watching him shut my door
something so feminine sinking to the floor
something so feminine not fighting anymore
something so feminine swallowing the pain
something so feminine whispering his name
something so feminine a love turned to dust
something so feminine learning not to trust
something so feminine standing up tall
something so feminine after all

Language of Love

when you are three, you draw stick figures on pieces of paper and hand it to your parents for it to be displayed on the kitchen refrigerator. when you are six you attempt to make breakfast for your mother on saturday morning, which you utterly fail at. when you are nine, you sit next to your father and help as he fixes another broken remote. when you are 12 you try to write a letter for your best friend and leave it at her desk for her to read. when you are 15 you tell your friend "text me when you reach home okay?" as they sit in a car, driving off. and when all else fails, when the stick drawing eventually falls off the refrigerator door, when the breakfast burns up, the letter doesn't fit the entirety of your mind's thoughts, when your friend forgets to text you they reached, when all else fails, you look at the people you love. your parents, your friends, your family, and with the same look in your eyes, that didn't change from five to fifteen, you say "i love you." and that, in my opinion, is the language of love. because "i love you" isn't a phrase, it isn't 3 words, 8 letters, a sentence. it's an oath, a pledge and even when you never knew the weight of a few words and syllables, somehow, you always found a way to let your people know you loved them. that is the language of love, it always means "i love you" and you don't have to say it for them to know it.

Favorite Song

as a kid, when my favorite song played on the radio, i spent the whole time anxiously analyzing when the song would end. i focused so much on when the song would end, that i forgot that i should enjoy the song too.

i have been doing this since i was a kid. i did this in my relationships, my experiences and my whole life. i never learnt how to enjoy or live in the moment. since i was a kid, i was always so hyper fixated on the anxiety around the ending that i nearly always forgot that the process is something to take too. over the years, i have seen this anxiety creep into my relationships. every person i ever talk to, i get nervous about them leaving and i get anxious thinking about their absence. absence has always scared me. i dislike absence. so even if that absence is of my favorite tune or my favorite human, i hate absence.

A Burnt Child

a burnt child loves fire
in the flames
cages they can't break
a burnt child yearns
the water he shall never find
and in the midst of nights
when he sits alone
palms of his,
he looks at,
swollen with feelings
he couldn't show
but a burnt child
loves his fire
so he picks his pen
to once more,
justify his sanity
with words
that never seem enough
flames on paper
scars from the fire
the burnt child admires

Lessons With the Moon

and when it's night again,
i think i'll sit with one less friend.
then,
i'll gaze at the sky,
search for her tender shine,
tell her all the world's hurt
and ask her mine.
dear moon,
do you still love the sun?
even when he's right there
burning in your sky,
but never to stay?
do you miss him
in the hours he forgets to turn back,
when the sky forgets
to let you meet?
do you miss him
in the spaces between light,
in the silence he leaves behind?
do you ever beg the sky
for a longer eclipse?

for just one moment
of quiet closeness
to admire a love you were never meant to have
or have you learned
to love him
in absence
as if presence
was never yours
to ask for?

What Actually Haunts You

what if i told you
it is not the person
who haunts you
it is not the person
who keeps you up at night
because it is not the person
that haunts you
it is the goodbye
you never got to understand
the person can't rip you
because they left
but the goodbye can
because it stayed.

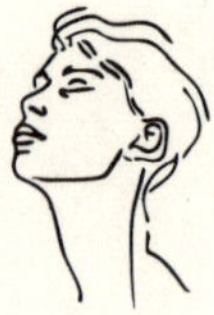

The Ability to Make Grown Men Cry

weep and cry
in my arms, you fall
the ability to make grown
men cry
tears rest on my shoulder
held it in till he could no longer
oh the ability to make grown men cry
see you swell
with words you'd never say
watch your tongue twist
with sentences his mind can't frame
so when mother calls home
he wipes his cheeks, tears they can't see
his skin didn't even feel
so then he goes
out to lie
the ability to make grown men cry
oh god.
the ability to make grown men cry
weep and swell, with words and tears
i see the grown men cry.

Sensitive Child

you are, what the teachers call, a sensitive child. when you were five, you cried because you were alone in a classroom, you felt insignificant. when you were 7 you probably cried because the kids at school made fun of you, you didn't like it. when you were 13, you probably cried because you didn't want to. throughout all these years, teachers called you a "sensitive child." it stuck to you like the words of a poet to his muse. you felt it in your bones. "sensitive." what is being sensitive? is it crying because you were five and alone with children who made you quiet or was it you growing up not knowing if you cried because you was five or were you just "sensitive." you've heard this word from almost everybody growing up, never knowing if it was good or bad, i don't think you will ever know that. but being sensitive, the "sensitive child" were you just weak or were you too young to know how to love despite being sensitive? you are growing up now, and i hope you see, as a matter of fact, the "sensitive child" in you sees, you aren't sensitive because you cried, you are sensitive because you are learning to love right.

Flowers

for when the flowers wilt
even when the roses darken
i'll still look into your eyes
and hand you my heliotropes
so when the heliotropes swoop
i'll brush past you
place a carnation in your hand
so when the carnation isn't kissable
look at me and i'll send
blue violets your way
so when the violets grow weeks old
place, i will, a daffodil next to you
and when the daffodils aren't dear anymore
when i am not as dear and my flowers hold little value
i'll send a holly to you
i'll push my fern to your palm
and when death do us part
i'll lay all my flowers on your grave
so to remind you
when the flowers wilt
look to the garden i will grow for you

Silence And Absence

sometimes, you misunderstand silence for absence. sometimes, words aren't heard, they are felt, and you child, you are used to screams and rage and fury and loudness and i fear you mistake the silence for absence. there is silence in one's absence, there is silent absence and there is silence but not absence. words are sometimes more than what one's tongue mouths. an oath, a pledge, a promise, all can be said silently but not never said. silence, not absence because maybe if there were no screams in your frail mind, you would hear hushed syllables you never would believe because you are used to fury but dearest, silence doesn't mean absence most times.

Knowing You

i hate that i still know you
i hate knowing your favorite song
i hate knowing your name
i hate knowing your favorite verse
i hate knowing your eyes
because those things aren't just things anymore
they are parts of you
but even though millions can share
a million things with you in common
somewhere between now and then
i will still know you
and everything about you
will forever be "yours"

Dear Person I Left

dear person i left,
you do not wish to see me
something i very clearly get
but in my coarse voice
my shaky words that never seem
to be enough
i would like to remind you
somewhere between our eyes
i need you to remember
that even though my presence
has, in you, died,
i need you to not blame yourself
dear person i left,
i never left you
dear person,
i simply left.
never you, but i simply left.

Take Your Breath Away

so maybe
when we're thirty
we're sitting on our front porch
talking about when we were fourteen
under the same moon
we grew, my love
from fourteen to thirty
i hear your lips say the words
most dear
"goodness, you still take my breath away"
so maybe
when we're thirty,
rocking gently with time,
the weight of the years
settles soft on our shoulders
not heavy, just known.
we'll laugh about the nights
we spent tracing constellations,
how the world felt too big,
and our hands too small
to hold all that we dreamed.

but here we are, love,
from fourteen to thirty,
worn in the best ways,
hearts still unshaken.
and when you turn to me,
eyes full of yesterdays and tomorrows,
I'll hear your lips say the words most dear,
"Goodness, you still take my breath away."

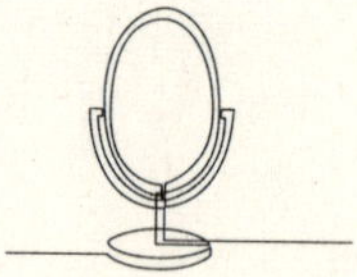

Reflection

when i look in the mirror
there's a reflection of you
when i look at my palm,
there's yours holding on so tight
tears down my cheeks
i can feel
your hands cup my face
scars on my body
your voice, the blade.
and i hate
how you're everywhere
and i hate it most
when you're in my head.

She Was Chaos

she was chaos
pure chaos
like the chaos of a painter's mind
or the chaos of rain
like the chaos of melodies she hummed
like the chaos of love and pain
like the chaos of the wild.
she was the chaos of midnight.
oh, what a chaos she was.
pure chaos.
she was my chaos.

Go with Grace

"if you leave one day,
leave like the fiercest storms
leave like the roaring flames
leave like the loudest crashes
i do not wish to live
knowing you left
any different than how you came
if you leave one day,
scream like the waves
dance like the rain,
go with all you had in your chest
if you leave one day
go with the grace
that you came with."

You Do Not Find Love

you do not find love
in the mirror
you say you aren't enough
"incomplete" you state
and through my most poetic quotes
those,
that i hold back when i look
into your hushed browns
you look to me
"why do you call me your moon?
i'm simply not enough, never complete
i do not glitter like the moon"
i hold back my words,
you see them wrapped around my tongue,
my love,
the moon doesn't need to be whole
to be loved.

Tulip

like a tulip in a rose garden
always the different shade in the palette
three seats but always the fourth
"it's okay"
you mutter, hushed and low
"i can stand"
just like you could stand
being the tulip.
the other hue
because you'd rather stand
than have to dance
all alone.

The Garden You're Growing

you don't plant a seed
knowing it will be a part of your favorite bouquet
you do, however,
plant a seed with hope
that it grows
into something more
than what seems to fill your empty palm
you don't look at the bud,
know it will be Persephone's descent
you do, however,
look at it with love,
you believe that it'll be far greater
than another hue in your garden
and in the garden you grow
you don't grow your plants
knowing it will be your unborn's harvest
you do, however, grow hope.
harvest affection. and feel pride.
because you never knew
what you could create.

I Can Feel It Choke Me

i can feel it choke me
it shouldn't
promised it won't
but i can feel your words
grip my neck, twist it and
leave my skin bruised
i can feel your gaze lock me
in my very feet, i can hardly see
my own palms as they quiver
shaking with vital truths that
they can't bear to hear
my lungs give out
the heart doesn't feel strong anymore
this one last bit
but i don't think you'll stick around more
i could watch you break
every thought of comfort i've had
i can't justify myself to you
i can't give reasons, my voice goes silent
and you hear, in my silence,
my world's crashing and breaking

My Muse

you don't have to understand
why i stop in every rain,
why i let it drench me,
soak me through,
until i am nothing but feeling.
you don't have to know
why open fields call my name,
why the moon makes me smile,
why the rain makes me weep
but know that it does.
you don't hear the whispers
that rise with the wind,
but my muse
oh, my muse screams for me.
it aches to be seen,
to be spun into ink,
to be stitched into melodies,
to live again
on pages and notes,
eternal and free.

The Silence

no sound.
quiet rooms.
i keep silent,
but my thoughts are screaming.
quiet rooms
where echoes should live,
but nothing answers back.
the silence deafens me,
presses against my ribs,
fills the spaces where words should be.
and these quiet rooms
they do not comfort me.
they do not hold me.
they curse me.
walls that know my secrets,
floors that creak beneath my pacing,
shadows that stretch but never speak.
i close my eyes,
but the silence lingers,
a weight, a whisper,
a presence i cannot escape.

It's Always Shakespeare

it's always Shakespeare
never Juliet
it's always the pen
never the page
it's always the singer
never the beloved
it's always the glass
never the whiskey
it's always the roof
never the home
and it's always the poet
never the poem.

I'll Still Keep One Page

i've lost count of days, my dear.
and i'm still here
drawing you into lines of poetry
we started writing together
and even though you have left me
to finish alone
i'll still keep one page empty
for the day you return
i'll still keep one bottle of ink
and a spare pen
for the day you want to write with me
once again.
and if that day weren't to come
for the next century or so
i'd still keep one page for you
because i'd still have hope.

For Once

for once
i wish you'd kiss me,
not as an apology,
but as a promise.
i wish you'd hold me,
not as a bandage to
your bleeding guilt
you can't rest
but as comfort to your heart
for once,
i wish you wouldn't rush every moment
because you know it's going to end
for once,
i wish you could be
almost
as selfish as me
and want to keep me too.

The Way You Do

no one fills four walls and a roof
the way you do
no one fills the pupils
of my eyes
the way you do
no one gets me to fill
pages of poetry
of second-long interactions
the way you do
and maybe that's why
no one fills the void in my heart
the way you do.

We Became Just Like Them

with my father's
inability to communicate
and my mother's
inability to leave
we became just
like my parents
didn't we?
all our fears
swore we wouldn't even go near
well would you look at that
with my broken armor
and your unnoticed wounds
we became just like them.

I've Got My Mother's Eyes

i've got my mother's eyes.
the same eyes.
dusty brown and sparkles
i've got my mother's eyes.
but sometimes
through my dusty browns
i see her too.
somewhere lost,
i see her.
i've got my mother's eyes
but sometimes
for even just a second,
i grab her soul
and i'm able to hear stories
she never told.

Thank You to Myself

thank you to myself. thank you because you made it. thank you because you deserve it. because you need it. thank you to every part of my body. thank you to my legs for getting me up each time I fell. thank you to my hands for wiping each tear off my cheeks, thank you to my lips for saying "i love you's" till they would swell. thank you to my eyes for capturing every beautiful and somber moment. and thank you to my smile for coming back each time i thought it'd leave. thank you to myself. thank you to that little girl inside me that falls in love much faster than i do and the little girl that loves to love. thank you to my heart for feeling so much. thank you to my heart for being so pure and not going numb when times were tough. thank you for leaving chapters unfinished and quotes undone and being at peace with pages you didn't fill. thank you for every tear, every ugly laugh, for every cringe joke, for every mistake, for every single time you were early to every time you were late. thank you for the utterly bitter coffee you make and the burnt toast no other human would eat. thank you for feeling happy at small moments when you found your favorite lip gloss or when your hair looked better. thank you for every rain you sang in but also, thank you to taylor swift for making such songs that i screamed till my throat went sore. thank you. thank you for letting me feel and every heartbreak you endured to shape me.

Forever

i hate that word
"forever"
i hate it because
i've heard so many lies
never once cared to believe
but a forever with you
is the only lie
i'd believe in.

Give Me a Minute

give me a minute
i know you're leaving
your foot is almost out the door
so please,
give me a minute.
just one more.
so i can feel your touch
and feel your presence
give me one last minute
next to you
till all you become
is another lesson.

April Mornings

April mornings used to be our favorites
at least we had something to look forward to,
before we turned into this big catastrophe
neither of us want to look back on
but as we pass by each other
not so much as a mere glance
as if we are just two complete strangers
the mature me, who realized
we are too broken to fix
lets you pass
but the immaturity,
pathetic immaturity
urges to fix it.

If Ghosts Are Real

if ghosts are real,
do you still see mine
at our spot
and when people have the audacity
to fill the halls
we once walked through
fill each corner of our corridors
with their loud voices
do you still hear mine?
a sigh.
a whisper.
if ghosts are real
do you ever wish
to be haunted by mine?

I Hate Being Alone

i hate being alone
because others voices can't drown
these loud thoughts
they pound
my brain and rip each nerve
till i'm bled dry
i hate being alone
and i think i finally know why
because it takes
a hundred people
to fill a void
for the one who never stayed.

Whisper

you whisper
and we stand in clamor
hushed and quietly
but i love loudly
so i never understood
your whispers
mistook them for absence of love
but
love was present.
for the first time,
just,
in silence.

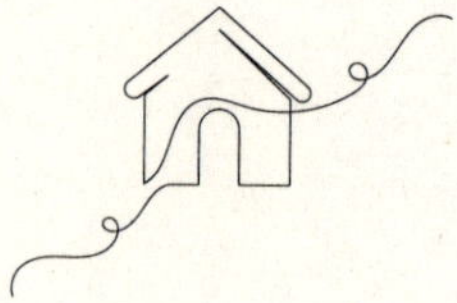

Home

if you came home
just four walls and a roof
i'd make you a hot cup of coffee
and you'd see
home is in fact four walls and a roof
but i am those four walls
holding everything together
i am the roof and i make a home
four walls and a roof
not out of cement and bricks
but a girl who learnt how to be a home

Art

art is beautiful
but it doesn't mean
art has to be perfect
art is beautiful
and beautiful doesn't mean perfect
you're art
and just to be beautiful
you don't have to be perfect.

Love?

you want to love?
so you're brave, i see.
wanting to love again
you want to be loved?
you think that
if maybe you love enough
you'll be capable to be loved back?
you want to love?
again?
try finding a new home
in new eyes?
you want to love?
so maybe you'll be loved back this time?

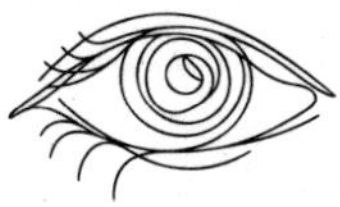

Hazel Eyes

hazel eyes says he cares
but i know
how hazel eyes looks when he cares
but looking at hazel eyes
getting lost in his smile
twisted lies
i never thought
i'd have to learn
how hazel eyes looked
when he didn't.

You Are My Home

you are my home
i get lost often
roads leading to nowhere scare me
and i get lonely often
but when i run even furthest
days i can't see my way back from
you are my home
and even on my darkest night
i feel astray
like i have nothing
i come home
to you
the only thing i'll ever truly own.

Small Things

small things you do
your smile after seeing me
your tracing of fingertips
till your hand meets mine
the look in your eyes
small things you do
the letters you write
and the poems you carve
and sending me lyrics of songs
we call “ours”
small things you do
pull me close in crowds
and break my doubts
it’s how i fell in love
small things you do
that are only so minimal to you.

Mad Man

it's silly what poetry
can make of a man
how tiny metaphors
tiny scattered bits of literature
install themselves
on dusty windows,
in knots of my shoelace,
in the still water in the sink
it's silly, truly what rhyme and words
i like to call mine
can make of a dull world
the world becomes a poem
a muse and a poet
it's in every bit,
every human and every corner
when the nouns and sounds
i bound by the staples of a 1917 notebook
spill themselves onto
dirty concrete and messy hearts,
it's silly, what makes a madman
so damn mad

Change

i have never liked the idea of change
it's the birth of something new
but death of something old
and a part of me
isn't able to let go
of the old
i hate the idea of change
because if something were to hurt me
i would find comfort in pain
and change
takes that comfort away
takes away what i'm used to
i hate the idea of change
because somewhere
i've gotten used to pain

1 A.M.

it's 1 a.m.
we don't talk much anymore
but they say time heals wounds
but at 1 a.m.
when i'm all alone
looking at my phone
waiting for you to call
it feels like time's not healing this wound
maybe making a few cuts deep
because it's 1 a.m.
i should be asleep
but i'm laying on by bed
your fingertips are ghosts on my palm
and i look at my screen
and you never called.

Goodbye

every goodbye reminds me of you
when we met,
i never thought
the word "goodbye"
would ever remind me of you
but now
as every person leaves
my thoughts chase to haunt you
and you kill me
a new way each time
as every goodbye ever said
screams more of your name
than it ever said "goodbye"

I Built Us a Home

i built us a home
out of words
we carved to make
our own
but these words and walls
aren't much better than haunted homes
i'd still say
"something died here"
i died here
waiting and pleading
for another second
where i had you near.

The Seat Next to Me Was Empty

i hate empty chairs
because they're never empty, no,
a ghost with a smile
i know
too well is beside me
and i hate how
the ghost looks at me
flickers in his eyes,
pulls my hair behind my ear,
grazes my skin,
like someone i knew too well
the seat next to me was empty
but all these ghosts
that linger in the void
of your absence
rob my solitude, then my sanity
i wish you could see
what your absence does to me

Clockwork

just like clockwork
you came back to me
each time you left
my heart so numb
i had known to fear not
because just like clockwork
you'd come back
but even the best clocks grow old
time forever frozen
broken beyond repair
and for the first time
i had taken my breath knowing our clock
ran out of forevers.

Falling Apart

falling apart
so rip me up
tear my heart
it was only ever yours
so break my bones
puncture my skin
your touch was all it's ever known
so haunt my mind
and every breath i take
i could never hate you
you were only ever mine.

5 Again

it doesn't hurt how you ignore me
it hurts how i react
because every time you walk off,
i am five years old again
crying and begging for love
and while you do a lot of talking
every time you leave
there is a feeling of doubt
"am i still enough to be loved?"
because i'm no longer the big girl
who knows what to do
i'm just five years old again
crying for her mom to stay with her
and not go.

I Love You

we both say "i love you"
but when i repeat your words
in my head,
it makes me question
for i always feel,
i love you and you are loved.

What Did They Teach You About Selflessness?

what did they teach you about
selflessness?
did they tell you
to rip off your skin
and shed for those you love
and run dry for the world
and did they tell you how to
build homes through your homes
and carve and etch names in your snew
did you learn that, did you?
did they tell you how
bones and skin and words and things
are small joys of man
and joys are meant to be given
did they never teach you,
how cutting off your flesh
will make you feel selfish for keeping your bones?

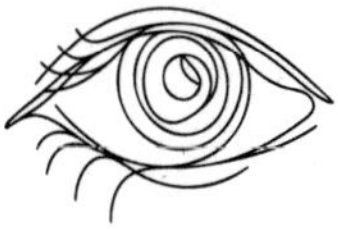

Glimpse

as i watch you,
like the stars
watch the morning sun,
i feel your presence envelope me,
you're close
but you have never felt more far.
i steal glimpses of you,
you're just centimeters apart
so close i could see you,
but somehow,
i only get a glimpse of you.

Pretty Crier

i guess after all these tears
i should be a pretty crier
after all the broken waters
i've wiped
i guess i should be a pretty crier
but every tear i dry
the redder my hands feel
as if there's blood on my palms
if only, this was not of any other
but of my own
i guess i should be a pretty crier
but not when these tears
stain my wrists more than blood.

Firelight

i'd lace together
my veins and skin
for you
if you said you felt cold,
knit warmth from the ache
in my bones,
turn my pulse into firelight
just to keep your shadow
from shivering.
i'd pull constellations
from beneath my ribs,
stitch stars into blankets
woven with silence and breath
a quiet kind of devotion
that hums beneath the skin.
i'd let the frost bite me
if it meant you'd sleep sound,
offer every heartbeat
as kindling for your peace,
my body a hearth,
my love a flickering flame

that never asks
to be fed in return.
if the wind ever weeps
through the cracks of your chest,
i'll build walls of my own skin
to keep it out.
and if the night forgets
to be gentle,
i'll press my warmth
against your spine
until morning remembers you.

House of Bones

i built a house from my bones
no brick, no mortar,
just the scaffold of ache
and the silence of marrow.
the door creaked like old ribs
and the floorboards wept
with every step you took inside.
you said it felt like home.
the walls were carved
with the stars i'd gathered
on nights i couldn't sleep
etchings only you
were meant to read.
constellations of every
almost, every ache,
every "i'm fine"
that turned into thunder
when no one listened.
you ran your fingers
over the seams of me,
where breaks once bloomed

like violets under skin,
where scars told stories
no lips dared speak aloud.
and still
you listened
to every brittle whisper
held between the lines.
the roof was stitched
from all the nights i bled quiet,
my spine the beams,
my heart the hearth,
and you,
the first to walk in
without asking
why everything
still trembled.
i built a house from my bones
and invited you in
not to stay,
but to know
how much of me
was made
just to be seen
by you.

Tangled Towns

we kissed like languages
that never learned to translate
your fire meeting my flood,
and both of us thinking
we could breathe in the smoke.
your name sits on my tongue
like a religion i no longer believe in,
but still recite
when the night feels too godless.
love,
wasn't it you who said
we speak in mirrors?
but every time i looked at you,
i only saw my own breaking.
our mouths were war zones
yours throwing stars,
mine catching them
like gifts.
we made metaphors out of each other's wounds,
and called it poetry.
and yet.

and still.
i remember the silence
after the "i love you's" ended
how it wore your shirt,
drank from your mug,
slept on my side of the bed.
how i spoke in past tense
but tasted you
in every vowel.
how even now,
if you whispered something soft
in that language only we ever spoke,
my heart would
probably
still answer.

I Usually Hate Myself

i usually hate myself,
looking in the mirror,
there isn't much I like,
you can say I hate myself,
every bit
but not the bit that lies in your eyes
i hate myself,
no doubt,
but I don't hate the part of me that lies with all of you
when I look in your eyes,
i see that part of me you chose to call
"home"
and you can't truly ever hate something that's not your own.
i would say I hate myself,
all of me except the part of me that's with you
that you chose to hold onto,
that you chose to love,
i don't hate the part of myself on which you chose not to give up
you call a part of me home,
you call it your comfort zone
and it wouldn't be fair to you for me to shower it with hate

so i save some love for it instead
i usually hate myself,
i hate the mirror and i hate my reflection
except the reflection i see in your eyes,
because the person i see on the other side,
is yours more than it will ever be mine.

Dinner with Religion

me and religion sat at the dinner table
i glanced at her skin frayed at the edges,
torn where hands had once claimed holiness.
i placed the wine between us,
and begged myself not to ask
if the stains were from other glasses,
shared at other tables,
or if they were pieces torn from her
sipped and spat by those who preached.
i smiled before i spoke.
i think that's when she shattered.
crumbled into shards of anger,
of ache, of sacred grief.
a blood too red to ignore
too loud to be forgotten.
but beneath it all,
i think she broke into love.
a love buried too deep to reach.
a wreck of all she used to be
collapsed across my wooden floor.
the table grew cold.

the wood, heavy with knowing.
and then
a red soaked into the grain,
a red too innocent to be wine.
and i knew it wasn't wine.
because no one
had ever invited her to dinner before.
religion spoke.
her voice cracked like old hymns.
and i held her
as she broke again
not into sin,
but into sorrow.
into something holy.

I Let Go of It All

i let go of it all
and have trust in me,
i wasn't weak for doing so,
i had the courage of resting my palm
and watch my pain slip through,
i learnt that holding on cut my skin like glass and dug holes deep,
so i let go,
for i know i have much more to keep
my love,
i have let go,
and dare you call me weak,
it's the strongest thing i've done in a while,
and i won't regret it,
till i feel my heart beat
i let it go,
for i was courageous enough to watch it fall and rupture,
i let it go,
and at least now,
it won't break me forever

Favorite Stranger

i passed by a stranger today,
i didn't even look them in the eye
but i knew their favorite food,
what made them smile,
and what made them cry.
i didn't even hear their voice but i knew my way around their skin like it
was my own
i knew their laughter
and i knew why they preferred being alone
i passed by a stranger today,
i didn't even feel them breathe,
but i stood there knowing i wanted their heart to beat
i passed by a stranger today,
they ignored my whole existence and i think i did too,
at least to their face,
but deep down,
i knew that they were my favorite stranger,
i knew there'd always be a part of me that would never even consider
them a stranger.
i passed by a stranger today,
i knew their favorite song

and i knew their favorite band,
i knew their favorite verse,
i knew them,
and the way they always sang along
i passed by a stranger today,
and i knew them better than most people in my life,
i passed by a stranger today,
and i remembered how once,
that stranger,
used to be mine.

In Another Lifetime

in another life, maybe
i'd meet my mother as a young girl
with dreams too big to tie down.
i'd smile at her and look
into her brown eyes, soft hair falling free.
we'd talk about love and life,
and she'd tell me things
she now finds too naive.
she'd say her favorite color was red
not because her husband said
it made her look young,
but because it was the color of her mother's lips.
she'd tell me about her favorite songs,
how she wrote them down
on tissues with pens she hid
in the bottom drawer.
she'd teach me how to braid my hair
not because her daughter would love it,
but because small reminders of love in the mirror
were hers to feel
she'd point to the scar on her body

not because she bore another soul,
not for motherhood,
but because she'd lived just one life
and spent too much of it living
to care about external hurt.
she'd tell me she's just like me
not because i'd be her daughter,
but because we'd be
two young girls
in a world
that never lets us be young.

I Will Never Be Known

i will never be a poem,
beautifully written and composed.
i will never be a song,
remembered and euphonious.
i will never be a novel,
coherent and captivating.
i will forever be the unwritten thought,
the half-finished story,
the ink smudged before it dried.
and i'll be much like the long-forgotten melody,
hummed once in passing,
lost in the hush of time,
a whisper on the edge of memory,
never fully heard
never truly known.

Let Me Lie

let me lie
let me say "I'm fine"
stop trying to read my mind
for i fear the day,
you read the right lines.
you read the right words,
you see my already initiated demise.
let me lie,
stop looking in my eyes in search for the answers,
stop trying to look into my smile,
where my sadness and my broken bones hide
stop trying to read my mind,
let me lie.
when you hold my hand,
stop trying to look for scars,
and when you hear the beating of my heart,
stop trying to find the end of it.
when i talk,
stop trying to break my voice,
find out what lies
between my words.

i stand here,
begging and pleading,
let me lie.
i beg you,
don't read my mind
for one day,
i know it,
you'll read the right lines.

I'll Never Be Your Favorite Song

i'll never be your favorite song,
i'll be the song you hear on the radio that you don't necessarily like
but don't bother to turn off,
i'll be like the shirt you try on but never really buy,
i'll be like the coffee you drink but never make again.
i'll never be your favorite,
i'll be enough to not be your most hated,
i'll forever be your second best
you'll probably be my favorite stranger
the stranger whose laugh i'll always be able to recognize
whose eyes i shall always seek
a stranger whose lips i'll always be able to read
a stranger whose scars may always bleed
you'll probably be my favorite stranger,
whose words i shall always cherish
whose thoughts, once my home, now seem foreign
you'll forever be my favorite stranger
and maybe we'll never share an inside joke ever again,
but that won't make a difference, now will it?
i'll forever call you my favorite stranger.

Thank You

and here you are, at the end of this book. perhaps by now, you and i have kindled a quiet friendship of our own. between the lines, the pauses, the petals and the pain, maybe you saw yourself too. this book was once just a piece of my heart, but now it's a piece of ours. a shared story, a quiet bond, and a proof that even in the most personal grief, love still finds a way to connect us. if these pages held you, even for a moment, if they made you feel seen or a little less alone, then *Letters to Gulab* has done what it was meant to do. thank you for reading, thank you for feeling, and thank you for carrying a part of her and me with you. this is not the end. this is a promise that love, even when lost, always lingers. it always lives on.